THINK to FEEL BETTER
A Guide to Mental Health

By
Thomas J. Blakely MSW PhD

Copyright © 2022 Thomas J. Blakely MSW PhD

All rights reserved. No part of this book may be reproduced or transmitted in any form or by any means, electronic or mechanical, including photocopying, recording or by any information storage and retrieval system without permission in writing from the publisher.

Twin Oaks Publishing—Belmont, MI
ISBN: 979-8-9868991-1-4
eBook ISBN: 979-8-9868991-0-7
Library of Congress Control Number: pending
Title: *THINK* to FEEL BETTER: A Guide to Mental Health
Author: Thomas J. Blakely MSW PhD
Digital distribution | 2022
Paperback | 2022

Dedication

This book is dedicated to my son, Thomas James Blakely.

Table of Contents

Prologue v
Chapter 1 Preview 1
Chapter 2 Personality Development 8
Chapter 3 Application of Personality Theories 19
Chapter 4 Spiritual Power 38
Chapter 5 A Process for Thinking 42
Chapter 6 Self-education for Self-intervention 46
Chapter 7 Critical Thinking for Self-awareness 52
Chapter 8 Attachment Theory 58
Chapter 9 Individual Self-worth 66
Chapter 10 Guilt and Shame 73
Chapter 11 Anxiety, Defenses and Addictions 81
Chapter 12 Feeling and Thinking 92
Chapter 13 Mental Functioning 107
Chapter 14 Relationships 117
Chapter 15 Examples of *Success* in Thinking 127
Chapter 16 It's Not Your Fault 134
Chapter 17 Getting What You Want Out of Life 140
Chapter 18 Crisis Intervention and Trauma 147
Chapter 19 Supportive Environment and Social
Role Valorization 152
Chapter 20 Obtaining Professional Mental
Health Assistance 161
Chapter 21 Chapter 22 The Last Word 168
A Lagniappe 180
About the Author 186

Prologue

Have you ever been nervous about something? Do you know someone who is anxious, scared; angry; disappointed; depressed or sad? These are just some of the feelings that people have when they feel things aren't going well. These feelings can affect the quality of life and can be tiring because they often require a lot of energy to manage. At times some may even think they are losing their minds.

The good news is that you can't really lose your mind; it's always there no matter what. It's the feelings that are bothersome and that you may wish would go away. That can happen with deliberate thought and effort.

The ideas in this book were developed over many years of practice in clinical social work during which individuals were counseled about a wide variety of emotional issues. The life challenges experienced by these individuals are likely similar to what you may be experiencing and may help you toward a positive resolution of your own life challenges.

This is the reason for writing the book. Contained within these pages are just some of the strategies employed with clients that have been successful. People who read the book will learn something about how to manage their own difficult feelings. Nearly everyone can find some resolution to the things that worry them or problems they have with others. People can find ways to adapt and function better if they understand the source of their problems and their sometimes inappropriate reactions to them.

Remember, it is *feelings* that are bothersome. People are sensitive to the words and actions of others, especially as children. Events within a child's life occur that can leave lasting impressions. Sometimes the resulting feelings are so strong they reoccur in some form on a frequent basis. When this happens, many people respond by not thinking about the issues and analyzing them in a way that changes their perspective. Most of them have not been helped to think about the assumptions they made about some past event or conversation that led to dysfunctional, worrisome or sad feelings. Many feel guilty about internal feelings but have little or no understanding about them. At times, these feelings can be so distracting that rational thinking may not be possible. There are reasons for that which will be explained along with other factors that can be real change agents. Learn to *think* about your feelings and find a new set of ideas that explain the circumstances around which the feelings occurred. This can lead to lasting changes in the way you adapt to the challenges of your life.

The themes of *teaching* and *learning* are central to this book. As both a clinical practitioner and a university professor, I understand the importance of effective teaching and adult learning. This experience has added to my understanding of how people learn how to respond to situations. In social work practice, education is an important part of the role of the clinician. As a professional social worker, I have taught clients about how to think in a way that is directly related to a particular psychosocial problem. Discussing child experiences and family relationships often reveals sources of anxiousness and/or depression that affect social functioning. Many adult clients have internalized a negative feeling about themselves because of feeling responsible for indifferent, neglectful or rejecting attitudes by parents or significant others.

Bringing these feelings to light opens the possibility of rethinking and relearning assumptions. People who think analytically about their feelings can gain knowledge about the effect of early developmental experiences in their later lives. This knowledge increases self-awareness which is helpful in making changes in feelings and behaviors.

As you begin reading the book, select a chapter that you believe might be interesting or that has something to do with your feelings. The book is not written in the style of a novel. Every chapter is independent. Significant ideas are repeated in various chapters so the reader will become acquainted with them even if a chapter is read out of order.

There is a chapter devoted to client stories. The examples given are taken from a number of cases so specific individuals cannot be identified. If a reader sees herself or himself in any one of the case situations, it is strictly coincidental.

The book has appeal to a variety of readers. Some will read it because they are looking for answers to puzzling questions about their feelings. Clinical social workers, psychologists and professional counselors may read the book for the suggestions and experiences that may be useful in their own practice. Some may pick up the book because the discussion of feelings is currently popular. Some may read it because the topic is interesting and features language and case histories with which they can identify and understand. Everyone struggles with their feelings at one time or another. Therefore, the possibilities for using the ideas presented in this book are virtually limitless.

Chapter 1
Preview

The primary purpose of this book is to provide a way of resolving difficult emotional issues by thinking rationally and realistically about those events occurring during a person's developmental years that generated negative assumptions and feelings about themselves. In order to develop a base for how and what to think, it is important to be acquainted with the basic theories about the development of personality and how these theories may be applied to resolve emotional distress. This is especially relevant to the kind of thinking that is recommended in this book. Reflective thinking can help a person uncover mistakes in assumptions and reactions to developmental events. The common theme of this explanatory approach is that childhood experiences are mostly responsible for how feelings are generated. You are what you feel but if you *think* you will feel better.

This chapter presents an overview of the content of the book. Its purpose is to give the reader a sense of what can be learned. Each of the chapters that follow concerns major ideas related to feeling and thinking, knowledge of personality theory, how personality is affected by life experiences, a process for thinking and factors that affect feeling and thinking.

Thinking about how to relieve emotional distress is clearer if one has an explanation about why it occurred in the first place. That is the reason for describing theories of personality development in Chapter 2 of which there are three prominent explanatory theories. Most people have heard of Sigmund Freud whose psychodynamic theory has evolved into the object relations theory that is in current use. Erik Erikson is known for psychosocial theory. John Bowlby developed attachment theory. All three can be labeled as "explanatory theories" since each of them focuses on childhood developmental experiences as the foundation for the development of personality. In all three theories the mother, whether called the primary caretaker, primary object or primary attachment figure, is the main relationship figure. A child's personality is shaped largely by the mother's nurturing care with the family and the environment as contributing factors. These theories are useful in thinking realistically about the negative emotional events of the developmental years. Bowlby's attachment theory will receive the most attention in this book. Freud's major ideas are presented as knowing something about them will increase the readers' understanding of personality development. Details about Erik Erikson's psychosocial theory are presented as it has practical ideas that readers can use as a guide to review their developmental history. Ideas expressed by Albert Ellis who founded Rational Emotive Theory also are featured. Ellis proposed that negative emotional events, such as those of indifference, neglect and rejection, may generate negative assumptions about the self and others. It is negative assumptions that need to be reexamined as to their true meaning. Rethinking assumptions can result in seeing the circumstances of the events were responsible and not the self. That change in perspective will open a whole new and positive view and relieve guilt and self-blame.

There are other theories about personality development that may be helpful if a reader is interested. For example, Carl Rogers and Abraham Maslow are in the humanistic category of theorists that are focused more on the removal of roadblocks standing in the way of individuals achieving their desired goals. Unconditional regard for the individual is an essential ingredient. William Glasser offers a similar perspective except that he proposes that the reality of a situation controls the outcome. Knowing something about Roger's and Maslow's theories can be helpful in analyzing feelings associated with a sense of not having been viewed with positive regard. Knowing something about Glasser's theory may be helpful in reviewing the reality of developmental events. Albert Bandura and B. F. Skinner are from the behavioral theory tradition. Behavior theory often is used in institutional settings such as juvenile or adult corrections or mental health facilities. It can be successful in improving behavior although it is important that anyone receiving behavioral therapy services internalize the value of any change if it is to be long lasting. The benefit to knowing behavioral theory is gaining understanding of what feeling responses have been conditioned in life that are not helpful in positive adaptation and social functioning.

Neuroscience also needs to be considered as there have been many significant contributions to the topic of personality development through brain research such as the function of neural pathways, neural networks and brain plasticity.

Chapter 3 provides more information about how theories may be applied to understand how feelings are developed from the experience of emotional events, especially those that are negative or traumatic. Ideas such as the development of consciousness, limbic mapping that is the process of storing memories, are presented. Several others concepts that provide the reader with a foundation for thinking about feelings are included. Reactions to indifference, neglect and rejection are discussed as these experiences during the developmental years have the most effect on personality development.

Chapter 4 is about the power of the human spirit. It is a reflection on the eternal existence of the human spirit that has within it a system composed of the soul, mind and heart. The spirit is instilled in every human and is a share of God's divinity. This system provides power to the intellect and will that is available to everyone when seeking to resolve emotional problems.

Since this book is about thinking a process for thinking is presented in Chapter 5. The process has three parts, context, explanation and thinking. Context is a review of emotional events and assumptions about them that occurred primarily during developmental years. Explanation is using attachment theory to gain an understanding of how these assumptions affected attachments to primary and secondary attachment figures. Thinking is using the result of explanation to relearn the reaction to emotional events to correct erroneous assumptions. Using this process has the potential of resolving emotional problems.

Chapter 6 further encourages self-education and self-intervention. It provides a theory base for the process of thinking outlined in the previous chapter. Chapter 7 is about critical thinking that clarifies the thinking process.

Attachment theory, discussed in Chapter 8, is prominent in this book. Attachment to a primary attachment figure is inherent in every child. A secure attachment style is formed through the relationship with this primary attachment figure. The style is a basis for positive social functioning that is normative behavior acceptable to observers. Some children adopt an insecure attachment style that makes it difficult to establish good relationships especially in marriage or as a parent. Insecure attachment styles frequently are the basis of emotional problems.

A secure attachment style is one in which self-worth is significant. Chapter 9 on self- worth presents information on how to develop and maintain it. Religious belief is one pathway to self-worth. The Commandments are a guide for behavior that provides structure for maintaining it.

Chapter 10 is about guilt and shame. Guilt is a feeling that follows a behavior considered to be against moral order or that was hurtful to another person. Shame is a feeling of being a bad person. Both guilt and shame are defined followed by suggestions about managing each in a way that decreases emotional distress.

Anxiety, depression, the mechanisms of defense and addictions are explained in Chapter 11. The word "anxiousness" is used frequently in place of anxiety which is more of a diagnostic term. The term anxiousness better describes the state of mind for the anxious person. Depression may follow stressful events especially those characterized by emotional loss such as the death of a family member or significant other. Addictions were included because so many people turn to social drugs such as marijuana, prescription drugs and alcohol as ways to "medicate" their anxiousness or depression These behaviors almost always lead to worse problems especially since these substances affect physical health and under some circumstances can cause death. It is imperative to realize that when addiction becomes a problem it cannot be managed successfully without professional help.

Defense mechanisms contribute to maintaining the balance between the parts of the mind and reality. Their purpose is to control anxiety and the dysfunctional behavior that often accompanies it. Defenses are automatic and do not require thinking. However, defenses do not solve the problem that generated the anxiousness in the first place, but when they are successful they manage it well enough so the person can function reasonably. If the defenses are working then they are fulfilling their purpose. Removing them may result in the underlying anxiety returning. Then emotional problems will reappear. When the defenses are not working, consulting a mental health professional is advised. A professional has the knowledge and skill to assist in resolving the cause of the anxiousness so the defenses are not necessary. Note that the effects of counseling or psychotherapy are typically not instantaneous and may take some time to be effective.

Feeling and thinking and the difference between them are the subject of Chapter 12. It is proposed that one cannot feel and think at the same time and that most feelings are normal because they were learned through experience. Details about feeling and thinking are covered. Thinking can clarify feeling and change behavior.

Thinking is a defense that works. For example, if one feels negative about self and has spontaneous negative thoughts, it is essential to think about whether these thoughts conform to reality or if they are leftover from child experiences from which erroneous assumptions were made about self-worth. Concentrate on a review of strengths including those many things that one does well and the many skills expressed in everyday living. If one thinks about the positive aspects of self, anxiousness may be decreased.

Chapter 13 is about mental functioning. It begins with a description of Freud's structure of the mind, ego, superego and id. Thomas Harris's concept of adult ego, parent superego and child id may be easier to understand. In the Harris model, the parent is the rule setter and the reminder of what behavior is right or wrong. The child wants what it wants regardless of the rules. The adult is the mature and rational part that manages behavior largely as a mediator between the child and the parent. When the parent is rigid and unbending about judgments regarding behavior a child may become rigid regarding behavioral decisions and find it difficult to have a "good time." When the child is dominant, the individual is selfish and demanding and their behavior often is described as "childish." The adult is a mature thinking part whose feelings are under control and with whom a meaningful conversation is possible. This theory is sometimes used by mental health professionals. It may be helpful to readers as they use the model for thinking that is described in Chapter 5.

Relationships are discussed in Chapter 14. They are an inherent need in all persons. The capacity to form relationships is related to the nature of the relationship with the primary attachment figure, usually the mother. The child gets a sense of a positive self from that relationship. The saying "birds of a feather flock together" often applies to relationships. Choose your friends carefully and your marital partners well. Guide your children regarding forming relationships. Keep the lines of communication open with them so they feel comfortable in talking with you about their friends and what is happening with them.

Chapter 15 contains stories about how individuals have been successful in using the process for thinking as a way to resolve emotional problems. These are stories about how one may use the thinking process described in Chapter 5 without a counselor. It is a process of reflection, self-awareness and thinking. It may not be completely successful for some individuals in some situations. In those instances a mental health professional may need to be consulted.

"It's Not Your Fault" is the title of Chapter 16. The main idea here is that children often blame themselves for the lack of attachment to primary and secondary attachment figures. Indifference, neglect, or rejection by attachment figures may make self-blame more intense. The result may be the development of a negative self. These feelings are stored in the emotional center of the brain and continue to influence social functioning in problematic ways. The real truth is that an erroneous assumption of self-blame was made at the time of the negative emotional experience. Therefore it's not your fault because you were reacting the way children usually react.

Chapter 17 is about ways to think and feel to get the most out of life. Thinking about assumptions and feelings really works. It can be a rewarding review of emotional events and the reactions and assumptions that followed to process and relearn the erroneous assumptions that were made at the time. There are several suggestions about what one may consider as ways to get the most out of life.

Crisis intervention and trauma are discussed in Chapter 18. They are described along with suggestions about what needs to be done to manage both. Many individuals experience emotional problems that generate a crisis or are traumatic or have resulted in post traumatic stress disorder (PTSD). These conditions may be relieved somewhat by clear thinking, but professional intervention usually is necessary.

Chapter 19 is a discussion of the concepts supportive environment and social role valorization. A supportive environment is one that protects a person from threats to resilience and overall development. It validates and encourages involvement and participation in whatever a person is doing. The term can be applied to a number of situations such as family or business. Validation occurs initially through positive emotional messages from the primary and secondary attachment figures. Feeling validated promotes self-esteem. Social Role Valorization (SRV) is about quality of life.

Knowing where to get help with emotional problems is important. This information is provided in Chapter 20. There are many resources available. If you have health insurance you may choose to see a psychiatrist, psychologist, social worker or nurse specialist. You may have a deductible that will have to be met before insurance will pay these providers. There are private agencies in larger cities that will make pay arrangements if needed. There also are public mental health systems in most counties where services are free if one qualifies. Finally, in many locations one can dial 211 on the telephone for information about where to go for assistance.

Chapter 21 is a summary of the complete book. It is similar to this preview chapter except the focus is on what one learned through reading. After reading this chapter the reader may more clearly see that this book is written in a way that any chapter may be selected to read depending on the reader's interest.

Perhaps readers can learn a way to resolve distressful emotions by thinking about the ideas in this book. For many readers using this information may help develop sufficient self-awareness that adaptation and social functioning will improve considerably. There still may be some emotional problems that require professional mental health intervention. If so, don't hesitate to get it. In those instances what one has learned about how feelings develop and how thinking can change them and change behavior may facilitate the treatment process. Remember, you are what you feel but if you think you may feel better.

Chapter 2
Personality Development

Personality is defined as the makeup of an individual's way of feeling, thinking and behaving. This chapter presents the ideas of prominent theorists who have written about personality.

The commonly accepted categories of theories concerning assessment and treatment of emotional disorders are: *psychoanalytic*, *humanistic* and *behavioral*. Sigmund Freud is regarded as the father of modern psychoanalytic theory while John Bowlby created attachment theory and Erik Erikson the concept of psychosocial developmental theory. Both Bowlby and Erikson take their ideas from psychoanalysis. Abraham Maslow created an ordered hierarchy of need. Carl Rogers is known for person centered theory and William Glasser for reality theory. Maslow, Rogers and Glasser are known as humanists. Pavlov, John Watson and B.F. Skinner are considered prominent behaviorists.

A theory that involves thinking and known as *rational emotive theory* was advanced by Albert Ellis. This is not categorized as a theory of personality development but it is discussed in more detail as it is directly related to the need for thinking as one way to resolve emotional problems. Neuroscience is also described as there have been many significant contributions on the topic of personality development through brain research including the function of neural pathways, neural networks and brain plasticity. Behavioral theory is significant for many in the assessment and treatment of emotional disorders, although it is not specifically a personality theory.

Sigmund Freud, with psychoanalytic theory, suggests that personality develops during childhood and is critically shaped through a series of five stages of development: oral, anal, phallic, latent and genital. During each of these stages, a child is presented with a conflict between biological drives and social expectations. Successful resolution of these internal conflicts leads to mastery of each developmental stage and to a mature personality. Resolution of conflict is partly based on the individual's ego functions. These ego functions are essential in homeostasis (balance) between the parts of the mind as a person lives and adapts.

The id, ego and superego are all parts of Freud's structure of the mind. Freud proposed that the energy of this structure was contained in the id, meaning that the conscious part of the ego, the "self" part of the mind, receives its energy from the id. The id, much of the ego and the superego, except for the conscience that is the voice of right and wrong, are parts of the unconscious mind. Therefore the treatment of emotional disorders must necessarily have been focused on the id. This is the primary aim of psychoanalysis as advanced by Freud.

Freud believed that people could be helped to recover from emotional problems leading to self-awareness or insight by making them conscious of their unconscious thoughts and motivations. The aim of psychoanalytic therapy is to release repressed emotions and experiences making the unconscious conscious. Unconscious instincts, thoughts and desires are part of the id.

The id is the unorganized part of the structure that contains basic, instinctual drives. It is the source of wants, desires, and impulses in addition to the sexual and aggressive drives. It is governed by the pleasure principle that seeks the satisfaction of impulses and instincts. As there is no reason to its organization, opposites can exist side by side in the id. Most of what is known about the id comes from trained professional observers of individual behavior, psychoanalysis, dreams and slips of the tongue.

The ego is governed by the reality principle. It attempts to satisfy the id through realistic ways and to mediate between the id and reality. The reality principle enables a person to delay immediate gratification and to function effectively. The ego is the organized part of the structure that includes the defenses, perceptions, thinking, and decision making functions. Conscious awareness is half of the ego. One quarter of the remaining ego is devoted to the preconscious where many memories are stored. The remaining quarter of the ego is unconscious.

The word "ego" initially meant self, but later came to mean ego functions. The ego determines reality and organizes thinking through ego functions. Conflict may develop from realistic anxiety arising from the expectations of the external world, moral anxiety arising from the super-ego and neurotic anxiety arising from the demands of the id. Anxiety affects adaptation and social functioning. For this book adaptation is defined as successful management of impulses and instincts and interpersonal relationships. Social functioning is defined as normative behavior in social situations, meaning behavior that observers would approve.

The super-ego is the internalization of cultural rules, mainly as taught by parents and significant others including religious organizations. The super-ego seeks socially appropriate behavior while the id seeks instant self-gratification. The super-ego controls our sense of right and wrong. It is an internalization of the father figure and cultural regulations. The super-ego that observes all the ego's actions may punish it with feelings of guilt, anxiety, and inferiority when it does not approve of behavior.

These are ego functions, meaning what the ego, the self part of the personality, does. At first reading some may appear to be complicated. Just remember ego functions are behaviors, including thinking, that are parts of social functioning Social function is behaviors observers accept. The first is reality testing, the ability to distinguish between inner and outer stimuli and the accuracy of perceiving both. Interpreting reality accurately strengthens a person's ability to adapt to inner impulses and external stimuli that contributes to positive social functioning. The second of the ego functions is judgment, the appropriateness of anticipating the consequences of emotional and behavioral expression. Good judgment also contributes to adaptation and social functioning while poor judgment often results in making inadequate decisions about behavior and thinking. The third ego function is the sense of self, self-esteem and an awareness of appropriate boundaries between self and others. This ego function is important in one's ability to feel good about themselves and to maintain necessary and sufficient balance of emotional closeness and distance from others depending upon the relationship. Control of affect (feeling responses), drives, impulses and instincts are the next ego function. This function is important in the engagement of appropriate behavior especially for those persons who tend to be impulsive in response to self-concerns and external events. Object relations is another ego function that was learned through experience, primarily with the primary caretaker, that objects (persons) are available even if not visible. An example is when mother leaves the room the child knows that she will return. A mental representation of mother has been internalized. The peek-a-boo game with children is another example. Notice a child's smiling reaction when the eyes are uncovered and the mother or other significant individual is revealed. This reassures the child that even though the caretaker is temporarily out of sight that person is not gone for good and will return. Thought processes are an ego function of memory, concentration and attention. Defensive functioning is an ego function of successful use of defense mechanisms that can be recognized through studying behavior and altered to meet behavior change goals. Stimulus barrier is an ego function of effective management of stimuli primarily from external sources. Autonomous ego functioning is the capacity to express ideas and feelings independently. The synthetic integrative ego function is adapting to reality and managing aggressive impulses. Mastery-competence is the ego function of performing competently in affecting the environment. In summary, the activity of these functions is an indication of the strengths and weaknesses of the individual's personality. They are one way to assess adaptation and social functioning. Sometimes people are described as having "a strong ego" which means the ego functions are working well.

Object relations theory is a neo-Freudian idea first described by Melanie Klein, further developed by Heinz Hartmann and promoted by Eda Goldstein. In this theory, the ego has its own energy system that is not dependent upon the id. This theory opened the way for direct contact with the ego. Ego psychology has become very prominent in psychotherapy because mental health assessment and treatment of the conscious mind is so much more accessible than psychoanalysis.

John Bowby proposed that attachment is a lasting psychological connection in which the primary attachment figure, usually the mother, provides safety and security for the child resulting in the development of a secure attachment style. Insecure attachment styles such as anxious ambivalent, anxious avoidant and disorganized result from a lack of attachment. Recall these styles are discussed in Chapter 7 Attachment Theory.

While mother is the primary attachment figure father , brothers and sisters also play an important role as secondary attachment figures. Negative self-feelings may develop in children when there is a separation, either emotional or physical, from the primary attachment figure or negative reactions from family. These feelings continue to seek expression and often are strong enough to result in non-normative behavior and/or emotional distress into adolescence and adulthood.

Attachment is a major factor in the development of self-esteem and self assessment. The core of personality development lies in family relationships. A person's ability to relate to others and to adapt to various trying circumstances and maintain social functioning depends to a large extent upon what was internalized in feelings as a result of attachment to family members. Other environment factors also have an effect such as gender, race and the surrounding local environment in which a person lived as a child and adolescent.

Newborns are totally dependent upon someone else for their existence. They must be fed, diapers changes, kept warm and comfortable and loved. Fortunately many children have a primary attachment figure that is responsive to their needs. They get "feeling" messages of care and being loved. They internalize these feelings and learn positive feelings about themselves from the child-primary attachment figure relationship. On the other hand those parents who did not have a positive attachment experience and adopted an insecure attachment style may be unresponsive to children's needs. This may contribute to children adopting an insecure attachment style with resulting adaptation and social functioning problems.

Father may be the primary attachment figure on occasion while siblings and sometimes other family members, are considered as secondary attachment figures. They too play a part in the development of the child's self-concept. Indifference, neglect or rejection from them may contribute to later emotional problems. Other attachments, such as those to other children or adolescents, also may contribute to a negative perception of the self.

Adjustment problems occur more frequently among persons who experience attachment problems early in life. Often these are expressed in parent-child problems and marital pair problems later. Sometimes reactions in emotional relationships are more serious and require medical or mental health intervention.

You may remember, without much effort, what your relationship with your primary attachment figure and family members was like. If your memories are dim or difficult, it may be that you don't want to remember as it would be too emotionally painful. Remember as you think about these things not to make judgments about them. That may be difficult to avoid but it's important to try as judgments often cloud accurate memory. It may be helpful to think of life as a process that one passes through with events that are sometimes disappointing or sad and sometimes encouraging and happy.

You may not know what developmental experiences affected your primary attachment figure and how that impacted the way she or he lived and reacted. They've had their ups and downs and may have struggled with indifference, neglect or rejection from their parents. What feelings people internalize about themselves has a long lasting effect. Your experience with these relationships forms a secure or insecure attachment style.

Working Models is a term originated by Bowlby. They are expectations and beliefs about the self and others established in the first few years of life. If a child feels bad and receives a prompt response from a caring adult, the child will learn the link between feeling and the positive response from a caregiver. Then a feeling of deserving of being loved will occur along with a feeling that others will be helpful when the need arises. A negative or uncaring response from an attachment figure will lead to an internal working model of the attachment figure as uncaring. This can lead to feeling worthless and may extend to expected negative responses from others. Caring produces a secure attachment style while uncaring is usually associated with an insecure attachment style.

Erik Erikson created a life-long stage development theory. It is a guide for discussing developmental issues and that is the purpose for using it here. There is some variation in the description of Erikson's stages. The information here is based on his original book *Identity Youth and Crisis*. Passing through each stage successfully requires the resolution of a crisis that is defined as a turning point in life. Lack of crisis resolution can generate emotional problems. The crisis of the first state is trust vs. mistrust with a sense of hope following resolution or withdrawal and detachment without it; the second is autonomy versus shame and doubt and the development of will with resolution or compulsive thoughts and behaviors without it; the third is initiative versus guilt with a sense of purpose with resolution or limitation of the freedom of expression without it; the fourth is industry versus inferiority with a feeling of competence along with resolution and inertia or limitation of action and thought without it; the fifth group identity versus alienation with a sense of fidelity along with resolution or social isolation without it; and, the sixth individual identity versus identity confusion along with a sense of psychosocial wellbeing with resolution or paralysis of social functioning without it. The lack of resolution of each stage crisis limits the ability to resolve the crises of succeeding stages.

Erikson proposed four adult stages of personality development. Resolution of the psychosocial crises of the adult stages and is based on the level of achievement of individual identity. Since most readers are adults they may use the information about adult stages to assess another adult's adaptation and social functioning which may be helpful in making a decision about a relationship or for other personal reasons.

Intimacy vs. isolation is the psychosocial crisis of the early adult stage during which successful marriage, work and lifestyle occur with resolution and social isolation without it. Generativity vs. stagnation is the psychosocial crisis of the middle adult stage. Productivity and creativity occur with resolution while unwillingness to be concerned for others occurs without it. Integrity vs. despair is the psychosocial crisis of the later adult stage. A sense of acceptance of responsibility for your own life develops with resolution with disdain for the weakness of others without it. The final stage is very old age. Immortality vs. extinction is the psychosocial crisis. A sense of wisdom arising from accumulated knowledge and mature judgment occurs with resolution and uncertainty and self-doubt without it.

Abraham Maslow developed an ordered hierarchy of five needs: *physiological*, meaning basic needs such as food, shelter and clothing; *safety* meaning security, *love* (meaning intimate relationships), *esteem* including a feeling of accomplishment and finally leading to *self-actualization* or the development of a person's full potential. The term self-actualization describes the movement toward achieving the highest of needs such as comprehending the meaning of life.

Carl Rogers developed a theory in psychology with its focus on unconditional positive regard. His theory is based upon the last of Maslow's ordered hierarchy of needs. He believed that people continuously react to their subjective reality or what he called the phenomenal field which changes continuously. The person develops a self-concept from this field of reality. Positive regard of others is the principal element in the development of the self-concept. While unconditional positive regard is free of value judgments, conditional positive regard is full of conditions of worth. People develop an ideal self and a real self based upon positive regard. These factors are involved in relationships. Agreement between the two leads to self-actualization.

William Glasser and his reality therapy focuses on realism, responsibility, and right-and-wrong, rather than symptoms of emotional distress. He believed that individuals experiencing emotional distress are in a condition of unsuccessfully acquiring basic needs rather than being in a state of mental illness. Glasser's reality therapy separates the person from the behavior and does not focus on a client's past or unconscious mental processes. Instead, the focus is on present behavior and the ability to choose a better future by choosing appropriate behaviors to achieve goals.

Because individuals are experiencing distress does not them sick but rather they are not behaving appropriately to meet their psychological needs.

Behavior theory is another approach to understanding self and developing patterns
of response to others with behavior as the focal point rather than on feelings. Forming and shaping personality is affected by the behavior of others toward us. Sociologists believe that humans tend to behave in ways that others will approve thus contributing to a positive sense of self. That said, there are a myriad of circumstances in which this doesn't work. We often don't know exactly what others expect so it's usually a guess. Children are born with what might be labeled a blank slate on which experiences are recorded and stored. This is why socialization or learning through the observation of others' responses and examples is so significant in personality development.

Pavlov originated *behavior theory* that can be traced to experiments with dogs and the discovery of classical conditioning. It was further studied by John Watson and finally by B.F. Skinner. Behaviorists believe that learning occurs through environmental stimuli. The practical use of behavioral theory is in the application of both rewards and consequences for behavior. Behavior theory is frequently used in correctional and psychiatric institutions to change and control the behavior of the residents and patients by establishing various rewards for desired behaviors and consequences for behaviors that are considered undesirable.

Parents of children exhibiting behavior problems may find this theory helpful. When considering the use of behavior modification techniques, it is important to explain the process to the children so they understand which negative behaviors will produce negative consequences along with those positive behaviors that will be rewarded. Negative consequences that reinforce the idea of not repeating an undesirable behavior are those that deprive a child of something highly desired. For example most children have some type of handheld tablet or maybe a Smartphone that occupies their time. Taking that away for a period of time is one type of consequence. There are many similar possibilities that will have the same effect. One has to experiment to discover those positive and negative consequences that are the most effective for their child.

Rewards for desirable behaviors are just as important and need not be either glamorous or extensive. Verbal praise for a desired behavior, as an example, might be quite sufficient. More specific rewards may be required for some behaviors with certain positive behaviors demanding larger or more extensive rewards. Control over the behavior will be easier to obtain when the limits are well understood so it is important for the child to know exactly which behaviors are expected and which are not acceptable.

All behaviors that receive attention tend to be repeated. Therefore some undesirable behavior may be extinguished or eliminated by totally ignoring it. If extinguishing or eliminating a behavior is desired, one should ignore the undesired behavior every time it occurs. Should a behavior receive repeated inadvertent recognition, the result is known as 'intermittent reinforcement' and can result in a strong call for repetition of the particular behavior. Consulting with a professional therapist who understands behavior modification theory and practice may be helpful for those attempting to manage behavior problems in both adolescents and adults.

Knowledge of social learning theory by Albert Bandura may also be helpful. For example, children observe the behaviors of people around them who they consider models. These models may include parents, friends, teachers, and others whose behaviors serve as examples that both adolescents and adults observe and imitate.

As a general rule, children are more likely to imitate people who are most like them and are more likely to imitate behavior modeled by people of the same sex. People around the child tend to respond to the imitated behaviors. If a child imitates a model's behavior and the consequences are rewarding, the child is likely to continue imitating the behavior as reinforcement increases the repetition of the behavior. Reinforcement can be both external or internal and can be either positive or negative. If a child desires approval this is an external reinforcement while feeling happy about being approved is an internal reinforcement. Children, adolescents and adults, tend to behave in ways that get approval. They can also take into account what happens to others when deciding whether or not to imitate someone's behavior. They learn by observing the consequences of the model's behavior. For example, a child observing a brother or sister being rewarded for a given behavior can be reinforced to engage in or repeat that behavior. This is known as 'vicarious reinforcement.'

Children tend to attach to models they perceive as having qualities with which they identify adopting their behaviors. A principle in behavior theory states that paying attention to a behavior will reinforce its repetition. That is one reason punishment often is ineffective because negative attention contributes to repetition. When children understand the rules and consequences they are generally more aware of their behavioral choices.

Rewarding good behavior is a reaction that promotes repetition of that. So being generous with rewards is desirable but can be as simple as praise, thank you and recognition. There are any number of reward systems or contingencies that can be set up with just a little imagination.

Albert Ellis, the creator of *rational emotive theory* believed that learning comes through experience. He proposed that some experiences generate erroneous and illogical assumptions. He also believed that people create their own disturbances. People upset themselves by believing that others and things around them are upsetting. People often say "you make me angry" when the reality is that anger is a choice and is often a response to fear. Children often have erroneous perceptions about the indifferent, neglectful or rejecting messages they get from caretakers that lead to concepts about their inadequacies which are stored in the brain. These concepts are mistaken because the perceptions that led to them were mistaken. However, these mistaken concepts continue to affect perceptions of self and others and result in continuing errors in both feeling and behavior.

Ellis offers a significant distinction between feeling and thinking. Characteristics of feelings are their forcefulness arising from previous experience such as intense physical reactions including feelings of pleasure or unsettledness such as headaches and stomach aches, etc. *Thinking* is based on objective facts, has a positive outlook in place of worry and if acted on assists in forming reasonable goals helping to prevent conflict.

The central concept in this book involves *thinking* and that can help correct erroneous assumptions. It can also enable a differentiation between appropriate and inappropriate emotions and between rational and irrational thinking. This can lead to more appropriate feelings. In other words *thinking* can change the feelings that accompanied previous assumptions so behaviors are more rational. *Thinking* precedes, follows and sustains feeling.

Remember, *thinking* may make you feel better.

Chapter 3
Application of Personality Theories

In this chapter how the theories presented in Chapter 2 apply to life experiences are considered. Categories of theories and the relationship among them is considered. Recall, the initial category was psychoanalytic and included Freud, Erikson and Bowlby. Freud was the creator of psychoanalysis. Erikson was a psychoanalytic psychiatrist and many of the ideas in psychosocial development theory were derived from psychoanalytic theory. Bowlby created attachment theory related to neo-Freudian object relations theory. There are common ideas in the three theories that relate personality development to a person's developmental history.

Freud proposed that early developmental stages were characterized by the organization of the structure of the mind and its parts, id, ego and superego. Successfully passing through Freud's stages of development affects ego strength and function. The strength of the ego, or the executive function, depends on how well each of the ego functions operate based on what was learned through experience in the developmental stages. If the oral stage is characterized by attentive care and nurturing, a child learns a sense of comfort about life and a sense of belonging. Indifference, neglect or rejection is the basis for anxiousness and feelings of abandonment that becomes imbedded in the personality and affects feeling, thinking and behavior, sometimes for years. During the anal stage, self-control over bodily functions provides a sense of confidence. This is a period of socialization during which rules of behavior are established. If these rules are rigid and applied punitively a child may develop a rigidity of feeling and a sense of being wrong that can result in inferior feelings. During the phallic stage a sense of gender identity or feeling comfortable with being feminine or masculine occurs. Negative responses from caretakers or significant others may lead to sense of confusion about self and related problems in developing appropriate social behaviors that may last for years. The latency stage should be problem free. If negative behavior occurs it may be a sign of emotional distress.

Erikson also proposed a stage related developmental scheme. Erikson's stages are described in more detail here because kit can be very useful in self-understanding. There is a crisis that needs to be resolved in each stage. The first stage is from birth to one and a half year of age. The crisis is trust vs. mistrust. The second is from one and a half to three years. The crisis is autonomy vs. shame and doubt. The third is from three to five years. The crisis is industry vs. inferiority. The fourth is from five years to twelve. The crisis is industry vs. inferiority. The fifth is from twelve to eighteen years. The crisis is identity vs. role confusion. Failure to resolve the crises in each stage can affect the successful resolution of crises in subsequent stages.

The failure of crisis resolution of the initial stage generates mistrust. Failure of resolution in the second stage generates shame and doubt; for the third stage guilt; the fourth inferiority and the fifth role confusion meaning uncertainty about gender identity. Almost everyone with any degree of emotional distress experiences some measure of each of these as they are serially related. Mistrust leads to shame and doubt that is followed by guilt and self-blame. Subsequently, feelings of inferiority develop because the individual becomes convinced that he or she is "bad." Role confusion, characterized by a feeling of "I don't fit in," occurs.

Perhaps a lack of trust rather than mistrust is a clearer definition for describing the development of personality and feeling, thinking and behavior. A lack of trust permeates the personality and those persons that have a lack of trust generally are apprehensive about many things. Suspiciousness about the motives of others and the expectation of a dismal failure of obtaining satisfaction from life often are present. Anxiety (anxiousness) has its roots in this stage. Symptoms of anxiousness include excessive worry about the future. Often oral behaviors are pronounced, such as talking too fast and too much, above average alcohol intake, smoking and overeating. Close relationships may also be a problem. There may also be a behavior tendency to be overly giving and doing for others.

Shame and doubt are the result of not achieving autonomy in the second stage. Children are walking around and beginning to be independent, learning how to do things such as putting on their clothes. When encouraged and supported in these efforts they become more confident. When criticized or not given an opportunity to express independence they may feel inadequate and dependent leading to a loss of self-esteem and feelings of shame and doubt that can persist into adolescence and adulthood. This is a period of learning appropriate social behaviors. If these are taught in a punitive way, especially toilet training, a longstanding negative sense of self may limit social functioning.

Initiative versus guilt is the prevalent crisis in the third stage. Initiative flows out of autonomy as children begin to initiate play activities with other children. When encouraged in these activities, feelings of self-confidence increase, especially in decisions regarding behavior. When discouraged, or subject to indifference, neglect or rejection, feelings of guilt and lack of worth may result. You already may have heard someone express a sense of guilt that cannot be traced to any past incident.

This sense of unexplained guilt is troublesome in many adults. This feeling often results from erroneous assumptions of self-blame that follow indifferent, neglectful or rejecting behavior by parents of family members. It is important for a person exposed to these behaviors to recognize these are the behavior of others. Don't make self-blame assumptions, It's not your fault.

Industry versus inferiority is the crisis dominating the next stage. This is a period when children seek approval from their peer group about behavioral and social skills and accomplishments such as those learned in school. Approval instills a sense of competence. Criticism, disapproval or an inability to develop a valued skill may result in a sense of inferiority.

Feelings of inferiority can make identity versus role confusion in the next stage more difficult to resolve. This is a major stage during which there should be thoughts about what one wants to do in life. Appropriate gender social positions and role behaviors develop. Successful achievement of trust, autonomy, initiative and industry contribute to identity. These attributes are the platform on which successful resolution of the crises of adult stages is achieved.

Readers can obtain a great deal of self-awareness by reflecting on their developmental history and thinking about successes and barriers to resolving the crisis in each stage of development. During this reflection, one may recall many feelings, both positive and negative. *Thinking* about those feelings can make you feel better when you recognize the normal mistakes in feeling that children make.

Bowlby's proposals about personality development are in line with Erikson and Freud. He centered on the idea that negative outcomes in personality are the result of inadequate attachment to the primary and secondary attachment figures and the subsequent development of an insecure attachment style. Bowlby was knowledgeable about neo-Freudian object relations theory which influenced his creation of attachment theory.

There is also some thought that development of personality begins during pregnancy during which the attitude of each of the parents toward the coming child can make a difference. For example, a planned pregnancy may have a different outcome in acceptance of the birth by both parents than one that is unplanned. Circumstances of the family may also have an effect on reaction to a pregnancy. These include the number of children already a part of the family, the health of either or both parents, financial ability to care for another child, especially in the case a single parent family, and the attitude of other family members including the extended family plus housing, employment, etc. These are all factors in the child-parent attachment relationship.

A newborn child is really helpless and totally dependent for care by others. A pregnancy usually lasts nine months. However, some children are born prematurely and some are born with birth defects that also may result in personality development problems. When these occur problems with attachment often are involved.

The emotional and behavioral reaction of the parents to these occurrences can make a difference. In some instances the child has to remain in the hospital while the mother is released. The period of time of separation between mother and child may result in anxiousness on the part of the child and subsequent attachment problems. Some parents may be overwhelmed by the birth of a child at a time when another loss occurs such as a divorce or the loss of a significant relationship. Parents, especially mothers, may feel overburdened by the birth of a child. This feeling that may be transmitted to the child who may perceive it as rejection. This feeling may be stored in the emotional center of the brain and can be a source of attachment distress later in life.

If the messages are positive the outcome is a sense of a positive self. If they are negative the outcome can be continuous and spontaneous negative thoughts about the self. Internalizing a negative self can lead to social functioning problems later in life. Aaron Beck, the founder of cognitive therapy explains this idea. He believes that children develop a core belief about themselves through either positive or negative messages they receive from caretakers or attachment figures.

Many young children who get negative messages are left with the conclusion that something must be wrong with them. There are two choices about who to blame for the resulting uncomfortable feelings, blame the parents or blame the self. Children realize instinctively that blaming parents will make the situation worse so they blame themselves.

How do children manage these self-effacing notions? It doesn't take much to realize that internalized negative messages may send children off in the wrong direction. They may find it difficult to attach to an attachment figure that is not very secure about a parent role. This can likely generate feelings of inadequacy and these feelings, when they develop early in a child's life, tend to remain into adulthood and affect adaptation and social functioning.

The child, operating as it does on feelings, feels neglected. You know how helpless and vulnerable babies and small children are. The negative feelings are overwhelming and internalized. These experiences are the foundation of feeling negated and aren't the type that will be supportive. They are negative messages and the response often will be a negative assessment of the self. There is a little child in all of us and it influences how we feel and behave. Those children whose feelings are not validated may develop serious personality disorders later in life.

The inner child, if it does not experience positive messages, will continue to try to fill the void created by the lack of positive messages. Children who are treated indifferently, neglectfully and/or are rejected may find it very difficult to get over the resultant feelings. It doesn't matter how serious the negative responses are and even a small amount can be damaging.

There are many circumstances that may occur during pregnancy and after the birth that affect the relationship between mother and child and the rest of the family. These may generate anxiousness that interferes with personality development and can affect a child's feeling, thinking and behaving. There are some children who do not respond well to nurturing care. The reasons for this are unknown but it is suspected that such a condition may be genetic. Mothers of these children may feel guilty and responsible. Often this will cause a mother to be overly concerned and worried. Engulfment, a condition of over reaction of protection and favor toward a child may follow. That may lead to a sense of emotional separation that also has the potential of increasing attachment problems and anxiousness. Mothers in such situations need to think realistically about the fact that whatever the reason for the child's reaction, it was not the mother's fault as she had nothing to do with the cause.

In summary, these ideas may be helpful to those trying to understand emotional distress using Bowlby's ideas. However, it is essential to be in touch with reality. Those persons who didn't have a positive relationship with either or both parents tend to blame themselves and internalize a sense of being bad. Ask what evidence exists to demonstrate that an individual is bad? If evidence cannot be given then one must realize that the damaged feelings of the child that are stored in the brain are controlling emotional responses. In these cases, one needs to differentiate the adult from child and behave accordingly. This is achieved by *thinking,* especially that a feeling of being bad came from a mistaken assumption. Remember, you are what you feel but if you *think* it can get better.

Maslow and Rogers were humanists. Glasser's ideas are similar. Humanistic psychology places emphasis on the whole person. Humanistic psychologists are interested in self-perceptions and personal interpretation of experiences. Choice, how one responds to internal needs, and current conditions tend to shape behavior. People are innately motivated to behave in ways that help achieve their potential. Therefore assessment and treatment of difficult emotional issues is not diagnostic as it is in the psychoanalytic tradition. Rather it is focused on removing roadblocks to the achievement of desired goals. Glasser's proposals are closely related. He believed that the reality of a situation eventually will determine a person's course of action.

Current neuroscience theory is that experiences, including those that are emotional, create neural pathways that are stored in the emotional center of the brain. These neural pathways affect future choices of behavioral responses to similar subsequent emotional experiences. For example, a child that is treated with indifference, neglect or rejection likely may feel uncomfortable in later interpersonal relationships because the stored feelings continue to seek expression. If a child does not experience a satisfying attachment to a primary attachment figure the probability is that child will experience attachment problems with other individuals into adolescence and adulthood such as problems with teachers, employers and friends. Awareness of these facts can be helpful in relieving guilt over feeling responsible for whatever indifferent, neglectful or rejecting messages were received from primary caretakers or attachment figures.

Neuroscience knowledge about the development of consciousness also is important. Any theory of consciousness must be in agreement with the experience of living. Personality development theories have not fully achieved this end. One explanation for this is the dominant concern about disease and pathology. This focus does not produce knowledge about how the mind creates consciousness. The fact that neurotransmitters and brain chemistry are so prominent in assessment and treatment of emotional disorders has contributed to the prevalence of pharmaceutical interventions. Unfortunately, medications may not be the complete answer.

A realistic theory of consciousness must include human nature and how the brain and the body are affected by it as well as how that union is organized. Assessment and treatment of emotional problems can be successful by focusing on deactivating those limbic circuits in the brain that are the source of the problem feelings. The limbic-cortical mappings of experience are stored in the limbic system which is the emotional center in the brain.

Successful treatment requires knowing how limbic-cortical mappings develop. They are conceived as generating the organization of consciousness. Metaphorically this organization is like a play. Developed during the developmental years this "play" if characterized by negative experience will formulate later negative responses to social situations and affect social functioning. Alternatively, if the experiences were positive then positive responses will occur.

This is why indifference, neglect and rejection during the developmental years can affect emotions for the rest of one's life.

The maps of negative experiences create dysfunctional coping mechanisms which eventually may lead to an emotional disorder. Limbic-cortical mappings support the concept of the physical basis of emotional distress.

The development of consciousness appears at about six weeks of age when the limbic cortex is developed enough to have a sense of self. This mapping of experience begins while the infant is in the womb. The limbic system develops further after birth in the relationship with the primary caretaker or attachment figure. During the early developmental years the child learns from the environment. The limbic system maps this experience and a more defined and organized sense of self and others. This sense of self increases and becomes more organized through childhood and adolescence with the limbic-cortical brain maps.

People with emotional disorders can recover because cortical mappings can be changed. Negative neural circuits may be diminished through lack of use and more functional ones established through new positive experience. A process of dealing with losing the old dysfunctional neural circuits is the beginning of change. One can develop a new "play." The new plot is one of positive response to self and others. Over time negative assumptions and behaviors will change. Symptoms of the emotional disorder will end. This is a process of successful psychotherapy that many people may have to enter to achieve a positive result.

An important factor in a child's development is ontogenetic endowment. Ontogenetic is a big word. It refers to the uniqueness of the self. There is no other person on earth who looks exactly like you or has the same genetic makeup, even twins. This is true of energy endowment too. The amount of endowed energy is fixed. It cannot be increased or decreased. You've noticed that individuals have varying degrees of energy, some less and some more. The endowment of energy helps some people to overcome problems that others cannot seem to resolve as well. Low energy people often will have a more difficult time solving emotional or thinking problems that require considerable energy to solve. When such things occur so much energy is focused on them that it draws from other systems that need energy. This can result is physical symptoms such as headaches, stomach aches or other symptoms of anxiousness.

This brings up something important. Whenever physical symptoms occur and persist for a while never assume they are emotional. While they may be, such a determination should be made only by a physician.

Words that express the roots of emotional problems are indifference, neglect and rejection. Everyone is helpless when they are born. A baby relies totally on the care of another person. If that other person, who almost always is the mother, has emotional problems of her own for whatever reasons, she may not have been prepared for having a baby. This condition of mind often results in difficulties associated with acceptance of a mother role. This can lead to ambivalence, meaning accepting and rejecting at the same time that can result in indifference, neglect or rejection. There won't be a sufficient attachment between the mother and child. The child starts life without the nurturing emotional support required for the internalization of a positive self.

Continuing indifference, neglect or rejection has a negative effect on developing children and adolescents. Sometimes children find it difficult to go off to school at first. This may be designated as school phobia but the real cause is fear of separation from the primary caretaker. This separation issue may be seen earlier in children if they become upset when the caretaker is unavailable or unresponsive to a child's needs. Temper tantrums often are an indication of lack of the child's satisfaction with the child-primary care relationship. Behavior problems in elementary school especially between the ages of seven and ten may be another indication of a child's problem feelings. Some children have problems with bowel and bladder control beyond an age when normal toilet training would have been completed. The presence of these issues may indicate emotional problems.

Adolescence may be a difficult period for some. Adolescents are breaking away from the controls and rules of parents and adhering to the mores and values of their peers. Reasonable structure is essential but they need to be a part of establishing rules. Keeping lines of communication open and working out problems and misunderstandings through rational means is important. If teens become distressed and unhappy they may seek companionship with other unhappy teens and this may lead to rebellion and a breakdown of relationships with parents.

They may withdraw and become depressed. If this occurs professional help may be required.

What one learns about themselves from their caretakers seems to have a long lasting effect. That is why mother is called primary caretaker or primary attachment figure. What one learns in that relationship becomes what one tends to expect from other relationships. If that relationship is characterized by ambivalence associated with indifference, neglect or rejection it is quite likely that the child will have doubts or difficulties in interpersonal relationships later.

These feelings are the result of lack of attachment to caretakers, especially the primary caretaker. You should have them as they are the result of experience. You know they don't work and you're uncomfortable. You will at first find it difficult to accept these feelings as appropriate. They are not your fault. However, that doesn't mean you don't have the responsibility of doing something about them. This is where *thinking* becomes so important. First you need to *think* it's not your fault and secondly realize that feelings about experiences during childhood will not work when you become an adult. If you believe you need the help of a mental health professional, get it. The physical components of emotional distress means medical and emotional treatment are required to obtain relief.

Often people who experienced indifference, neglect or rejection during developmental years have spontaneous negative thoughts about themselves. One must think these are the result of erroneous assumptions about what happened. Children make negative assumptions about self. They blame and feel guilty and bad and experience a loss of self-worth. They may think that whatever negative messages came from others were their feelings. If this is your experience it is important to know that it's not your fault. Whatever negativity others feel is a response to their own experiences for which you are not responsible. One should not turn over to others judgments about self-worth. Those judgments belong to the individual and are made based on an accurate assessment of one's strengths and weaknesses. Strengths are used to bolster self-esteem. If one has weaknesses they should be acknowledged and corrected. Everyone has weaknesses. They are a part of human nature.

Doing something about negative self feelings requires a great deal of effort. Memories of feelings learned early in life are stored in the emotional center of the mind and will continuously seek expression. The mind is a friend. It will automatically come to one's aid when anxiety provoking events occur by burying the hurt feelings. However, these feelings are energized and seek release that often occurs in hidden ways. For example, one may notice that certain situations and certain people stimulate anxiousness in a person even though one can't think of any reason why this should occur.

This may be due to a phenomenon called transference. What is experienced in the developmental years with significant relationships, especially parents, may be transferred to other persons. Transference is automatic and occurs without thought. Therefore, *thinking* about why spontaneous negative feelings toward others occasionally happen may be helpful.

Feelings are never good or bad or right or wrong. They are just feelings and cannot be judged. Often negative self-judgment is associated with feelings especially when those are confusing. An example is how one feels about another person with whom there is a close relationship. People generally feel that they must love their parents even when one or both parents have been indifferent, neglectful or rejecting. This is often based on the Commandment 'Honor thy Father and Mother. Honor and honesty are associated words as are honor and respect. The meaning of this Commandment could be that one should not behave dishonorably or disrespectfully toward parents. It doesn't have anything to do with whether or not one likes or loves their parents even though many people believe that it does. One may not love parents, or even like them. If feelings really are never good or bad or right or wrong, then you can be free to feel toward your parents whatever way you want without feeling that you are bad because of it.

Generally there are many guilt feelings in people who have parents that are indifferent, neglectful or rejecting This response is mostly because if the parent-child relationship was not satisfying, the child will assume fault. As mentioned earlier there are two choices, blame the parents or blame the self. Children are aware enough to know that blaming parents can make the situation worse so they blame themselves. Guilt arises and is sometimes so overwhelming that it interferes with social functioning.

These feelings may be very handicapping. Children can believe they are bad. This contributes to a negative sense of self that is accompanied by negative self-effacing thoughts and judgments. Realistic? No, but it happens all the time. Children in this kind of reactive mode find it difficult to function. They often become very anxious about themselves and how others see them.

Generally people behave in ways they believe will be approved by others. If there is confusion about what will be approved, unapproved behavior may occur that will generate negative response from others. This may result in withdrawal from others and feeling rejected and that generates anxiety (anxiousness). It also may cause acting out of behaviors and is a major contributor to delinquent behavior in adolescents.

One experience that occurs for some people is constantly "hearing negative thoughts in their heads." Where do these negative thoughts come from? The likely answer is that they come from stored negative neural pathways about the self that seek expression in negative thoughts like "I'm not good enough," "I can't do that," "I'm not very good looking," "I'm a failure," "People don't like me," and so on. These feelings, were established in the developing child whose environment was characterized by indifference, neglect or rejection. Negative responses from caretakers or other significant persons, if heard often enough, build an internal negative sense of the self. These feelings are very uncomfortable. They interfere with social functioning and may lead to emotional distress. However, this distress may be managed by *thinking* that the behavior of significant caretakers or attachment figures belongs to them. Don't assume their feelings define bad. Remember, you are what you feel but if you *think* feelings can get better.

A major source of negative self-assessment originates in the trauma of abuse. Abuse occurs in different ways; verbal, physical, sexual or emotional. Whatever the type of abuse, the results can be long-standing. If one was verbally abused by a parent the result may be self-consciousness and lessened self-esteem. This can contribute directly to viewing ordinary tasks as more difficult than they really are and to believing that others are less accepting and less friendly than they really may be. Physical abuse also is damaging to self-esteem but also contributes to ambivalent feelings about attachment to a primary caretaker or attachment figure. Anger, resentment and guilt may result in what is generally called a "short temper." Temper tantrums in children almost always are a sign of problems in the child-primary caretaker relationship. In adults it is frequently a sign of inferior feelings about self.

These feelings can make a person act as if nothing is wrong when it really is, display a masterful attitude that is false and disguise true feelings with "show off" behavior that can result in negative perceptions by others. These feelings contribute to withdrawal behavior. The really quiet kid in the back of the classroom is the one about which concern should be felt. These feelings may result in acting out behavior, difficult interpersonal relationships, argumentative displays and a generally negative attitude.

A discussion of feelings would be incomplete without considering the effects of abuse during the developing years. While there are a number of types of abuse, such as physical and emotional, sexual abuse is probably the most damaging to a child's emotions and invariably results in lowered self-esteem. If the perpetrator is a grandparent, the child may be very angry at the mother even though the child may never disclose anything and the parent may never know the abuse occurred. Feelings created by the abuse can set up a barrier that lasts for a very long time. The child may not tell a parent out of fear that telling would cause a strain between a parent and a grandparent. Often the perpetrator will threaten the child if anyone is told about the abuse. The child is confused about the role of the perpetrator but suppresses the confusion. Often the abuse occurs with more than one child in the family and this will lead to interpersonal problems among all the children. When the abuse is anal, retention of fecal material may occur. These conditions may require professional intervention.

It is important to realize that any type of sexual abuse may have an accompanying response of charged erotic excitement and simultaneous pleasurable feelings that can be very confusing, with the child unable to understand how an abusive act can feel good. If a child is told that nothing can change the pleasurable physical erotic sensations occurring with stimulation of erotic zones, that these sensations are perfectly normal, guilt often can be relieved.

There are mixed reactions to sexual abuse. Anxiety and depression may occur. Excessive feelings of guilt and being "bad" may occur as well as sexual frigidity or sexual promiscuity.

Difficulty in establishing and maintaining interpersonal relationships is a frequent outcome. When changes in a child's behavior become apparent suspecting abuse, is not unreasonable. Such experiences often leave an emotional reaction in their wake. It is very important that these problems receive immediate mental health intervention.

As was said previously, the mind is one's ally and friend and as such it may repress memories of the trauma of abuse, especially sexual abuse, so that no memory of it appears. That doesn't mean there are no indications of trouble as the energy required for repression cannot maintain it completely so disguised manifestations of distress occur instead. Sometimes it takes more than the available skill of the average person to observe these signs so repression wins. Often there will be triggers to anxiety or depression that don't seem to have a cause. This may be because memory of the event is trying to escape repression but is not obvious to most observers. Troubling behavior always should be investigated. Often memories of trauma such as those occurring with sexual abuse appear suddenly in adulthood and may require professional intervention.

The ability to manage the memories of abuse of any type is dependent upon the strength of relationships, primarily with parents. The internalization of a positive self is a substantial aide in management. Of course, if the perpetrator is a parent, this strength is not available. Many times the spouse of the perpetrator is aware of the abuse but does nothing or parents don't believe the child if told about the abuse. These may have a serious negative effect on the child.

Persons who have experienced any kind of abuse often remember that it occurred along with or separate from indifference, neglect and rejection by caretakers. Each of them tells a specific story about developmental years but all of them have a common theme that appears in their narrative; a search for acceptance. Most of these people don't accept themselves, don't like themselves and experience anxiousness and depressed feelings a lot of the time.

It is essential to see the difference between the child and the adult parts of personality. When children experience indifference, neglect or rejection strong feelings are stored in memory and can affect how they relate to others. There is a void that develops in positive feelings about the child self that continues into the adult years. This void is filled with a search for missing acceptance, a search for the nurturing caring caretaker who did not or was not able to satisfy the child's needs. The positive news is that it is not necessary for a person who has not been fully accepted to carry this burden forever. Acceptance or approval by a parent or anyone else does not in any way decrease a person's value or worth as a human being. Turning over to anyone the right to judge or determine self-worth is not appropriate.

A later chapter concerns attachment which is a theory about human relationships that is important for everyone to understand. Attachment styles are discussed in terms of their affect on children. This is about parenting styles that are formed as the means of managing the nature of attachment of the primary attachment figure. It has been written previously that newborns are totally dependent upon a caretaker for their existence. The caretaker has her own personality and her own issues and these will affect her attitude towards her baby. How the baby responds to the caretaker's care contributes significantly to the formation of the child's attachment style.

The family's attitude toward the introduction of a new member can also affect a child's attachment style. Factors in this include: the number of older brothers and sisters, the age space between this child and the next older and younger sibling, whether this child was planned, the mother's general health, the father's attitude toward having another child, the family income, whether or not the mother is employed and if she is the type and quality of child care provided and the attitude of the other children toward an added child.

It is important at the outset to know that an attachment style is a learned behavior. Therefore it cannot be judged as right or wrong only whether it works effectively to maintain social functioning skills. Differing attachment styles will affect relationships with friends and associates but especially those with whom one has an intimate relationship.

Individuals sometimes choose marital partners based on the other's attachment style. This is not a conscious decision. Rather it is a good example of the content in the chapter entitled Mental Functioning that discusses the effect of the unconscious on feelings and behavior. It was mentioned previously that "birds of a feather flock together." This is the opposite where a person is attracted to another feeling that joining with the other will create a union that will result in solving an emotional problem. This is discussed in more detail in the chapter on relationships. Suffice it to say that these relationships are rarely successful because they are on a shaky foundation from the beginning.

Caretakers of children have a tremendous responsibility. Having a baby can be a frightening experience for some and many do not learn about or understand the intricacies of parenting. In the current culture where many very young women are having babies without being married, the question of how they can learn to be a good parent has to be addressed.

Another factor to consider is the high divorce rate and how that results in the potential for indifference, neglect and rejection on the part of both primary and secondary attachment figures. Animosity toward a divorced partner often results in children being pawns in the hands of angry parents who use the children to carry out hateful actions toward each other.

The characteristics of the relationship between a mother and a grandmother provide clues about how the mother will relate to her child. There are many mothers who experienced indifference, neglect and/or rejection from their mother. This often results in internalizing negative feelings of inadequacy and low self-esteem. These feelings can affect her parenting skills and may lead to anxiety in her children.

Sometimes people decide to have a baby because they believe this will strengthen the marital relationship. Usually this doesn't work and the child becomes a constant reminder of the problems that existed even before the child was born. This can happen to couples that adopt a child believing they have an obligation to have children, or for some other personal need on the part of either parent. The child may serve as a reminder of the parents' inability to have a child.

The child will sense this and it may create an uneasy internal feeling.

The discipline and training of children is the foundation of the development of character. Character is defined as an internal strength developed through socialization that enables a person to clearly see the difference between right and wrong. It is different from personality that is the way we learn to present ourselves to others so we can relate effectively and survive in a world where there are many challenges.

Socialization is an important developmental period. Children need to learn the basic rules of relating to others to learn social functioning. They need explanations about the rules of behavior and the consequences for not following them so that when misbehavior occurs they know it was their decision. When socialization is harsh and punitive children may become angry and resentful. These reactions often will be followed by acting out behavior that increases the tension between them and their parents.

Those parenting styles that contribute to a child's attachment style are important. A parent may be unresponsive, critical or dismissive, inconsistent or frightening and confusing. The responsive caretaker is one that enables a positive bond with a child and attends to the child's expression of whatever need arises. This parenting style ultimately leads to a child developing a secure attachment style.

Previously we referred to neuroscience which is a multidisciplinary theory of brain function. It may be helpful to expand on this now as the subject is becoming more significant in mental health and in the resolution of emotional problems. One possibility is to supplement neuroscience knowledge with an explanatory theory such as attachment theory which can lead to an understanding about how these ideas may be used in combination to achieve positive mental health. Attachment theory is suggested rather than other theories because it can be measured.

Neuroscience functions also are measurable.

Combining these disciplines makes the relationship between attachment style, neurological makeup and possible later problems with social functioning clearer.

Although attachment theory is an example of supplementing neuroscience knowledge, other theories such as object relations or psychosocial development, will also fit albeit with modifications depending upon the theory.

Neuroscience findings, especially those concerning neural pathways and neural plasticity, highlight the contributions of physiology to the assessment and management of emotional disorders. The knowledge base of neuroscience is extensive and awareness of all its complexities is beyond the scope of this book. However, awareness of basic concepts in neuroscience can make a significant contribution to the ability to improve social functioning.

Neuroscience has established the existence of neural pathways in the brain that are generated through experience, among which are those related to attachment. It is these pathways within networks in the brain that contribute to social functioning. Neural pathways are a series of synapse connections. A synapse is a structure that permits a neuron (or nerve cell) to pass an electrical or chemical signal to another neuron or to the target cell. Neuroscience also produced evidence of what is labeled neural plasticity or the brain's ability to adapt and change in response to the environment.

Researchers described developmental experience as the priming of synaptic connections through relationships with caretakers. This means the system of neural pathways is affected by childhood experiences. The brain is a social organ that develops through interactions with others, especially those with whom there is a close relationship. These observations indicate a connection between neuroscience and attachment theory as the latter focuses on developmental experiences as sources for later emotional disorders and the former is a way of understanding and explaining what this connection means.

Many adults have memories of negative and rejecting experiences with one or both parents. A common reaction on the part of developing children is to wonder what's wrong with them that caused the parents to react negatively or reject them. This negative self-assessment generates a reaction that contributes to an insecure attachment style which is reactivated repeatedly in other relationships. A connection between attachment theory and neuroscience can be found in the storage of attachment experiences in neural pathways.

This leads to ideas that support emotional problems having a physical base. The child development experience is the priming of synaptic connections through relationships with caretakers. This means that maturing of the brain is dependent upon early attachment experiences that shape the brain and patterns of relating to others. The brain is a social organ that is developed through interactions with others especially with whom there is a close relationship such as parents and brothers and sisters or substitute primary caretakers. This strengthens the connection between neuroscience and attachment theory because of the shared focus on developmental experiences as sources for later emotional disorders and the understanding and explaining about what this connection means.

Attachment theory postulates that inherent within every person is the need to attach to a primary attachment figure. When the primary attachment figure is indifferent, neglectful or rejecting this results in an insecure attachment style. A neurophysiological fact is that neuropathways of these experiences are stored in the brain where they will continue to seek expression and influence behavior and feelings. Therefore, there are anatomical and physiological components of emotional disturbance with emotional problems having an anatomical or physical base. Many people may find this explanation more acceptable and explainable than the more abstract theories of emotion.

Another fact about the brain is neuroplasticity though this is not yet completely understood. Changes in the brain occur throughout life and new experiences can change neural pathways. This suggests that a person can relearn the effects of trauma and other negative experiences. This can be instrumental in change from an insecure to a secure attachment style.

Knowledge about neuroscience can be learned, especially about developmental experience forming neural pathways and neural plasticity making it possible to change the pathways with new experience. Knowing how the brain functions can provide a person with more self-control and perseverance in problem solving. Knowing about neural plasticity provides one with confidence that change can occur. Persons interested and willing may recall memories of child experiences that prompted the development of an insecure attachment style. Realizing the consequences of an attachment figure with an insecure base and how the affected emotions were stored in neural pathways may be possible. With this realization one can begin to *think* about the reality of feelings rather than allowing the feelings to influence behavior. This can lead to changes in behavior, new experience and new neural pathways. One may then begin to move from an insecure style to a more secure one.

In summary, this chapter has presented ideas about what happens when indifference, neglect and/or rejection and abuse occur in a child's life. It has provided an understanding of how behavior and feelings may be affected by early negative experiences.

Chapter 4
Spiritual Power

A natural spiritual power in all humans, the system of the spirit composed of the soul, mind and heart, is presented in this chapter. This system is a part of human nature as created by a Supreme Being. The Bible provides evidence that supports the proposal that the soul, mind and heart are a single entity within the human spirit.

Mental power can be helpful in achieving self-awareness. It has the potential of empowering a person to think analytically and clearly about emotional experiences as a way of relieving anxiousness about the self and others. One can recognize individual inherent strengths related to having a religious belief that God is the Holy Spirit and human spirits, in the form of soul, mind and heart are an extension of his spirit. Aristotle, the famous Greek philosopher, believed that every living thing has a soul although there are different levels of the soul. In Greek philosophy the soul and mind were considered as one. The heart is joined to both as it refers to the innermost aspect of humanity and the seat of morality and mental activity. The soul, mind and heart are parts of the human spirit that joins the human to God forever.

The body is limited in existence and is where the spirit resides for a temporary period. However, the spirit - the soul, mind and the heart - lives for eternity and infers that the spirit has an infinite mental capacity which enhances both the intellect and will. The potential of the mind is always present and has an effect on human behavioral choices. If one uses the power of intellect and will as properties of the soul, and listens to the positive nature of the heart, that would increase the mind's ability to resolve emotional problems. Spiritual power is the supernatural essence of the spirit that is available for this purpose.

Consider the meaning of infinity as related to time. Because there is no beginning and no end to infinity, it is not governed by time as we know it. Everything in infinity is present time. There is no past or future. God, or the Supreme Power, is not limited by time. The same is true for the soul, mind and heart as they too have an infinite quality. They share a divinity with God but do not share the essence of God.

This leads to a discussion of the purpose of human life. Considering this purpose is difficult without a belief in a Supreme Being. One may think about this scientifically. Biogenesis is a scientific concept that life comes from life. A child is born through procreation. An oak tree develops from an acorn. A flower grows from a seed. Because life comes from life the question must be asked about the first source of life. That first source must be the creator of life and as such has no beginning and no end. Such a being lives in infinity where the limitations of time do not exist. Since God is the creator of human life it is reasonable to believe that a purpose in life is to obey his Commandments. The first three honor God. The remainder are rules for behavior toward persons. The Commandments give order and purpose to life. Obeying the Commandments gives structure to behavior. Spiritual power is the quality of the system of soul, mind and heart that makes it possible to live life according to the Commandments.

A fundamental concept about the relationship between God and man is free will. Free will is a gift from God and is God's sharing of his divinity with humans. This is a significant aspect of spiritual power. This power is a concept that is important to understand, as recognizing having a share of divinity enables positive choices about how to think and behave. This is an empowering idea. *Thinking* can break the connection between feeling and behavior so behavior becomes more rational. Religious expression is based largely on thinking. It is important to assess one's feelings and thoughts about religion as a pathway to helping understand that spiritual power is available as a resource for resolving emotional problems.

The idea of the mind, the heart and the soul being parts of a dynamic system is very empowering. Recognizing the power of the mind's properties of intellect and will is important in self-understanding. Those persons who have a religious belief system recognize how the soul, mind and heart are involved in their everyday life. God is always present and shares his divinity with humans as we are created in his image. This idea reminds them of their basic goodness and potential control over the problems of life.

Attachment theory, described in another chapter in this book, is a theory one can use to explain some negative feelings about self and others. Fortunately most people have a secure attachment style. They do not have difficulty in adaptation which is defined as successful management of drives, impulses, instincts and interpersonal relationships or social functioning defined here as normative behavior in that is generally acceptable to observers.

It may be helpful to readers to review the behaviors of the ambivalent and avoidant insecure styles. The behaviors of anxious ambivalent persons are: approach avoidant conflict meaning mixed feelings about interaction with others, strong emphasis on getting attention, continuously seeking affection and support, compulsive approach to getting partners to meet attention needs, fear of rejection, doubts about obtaining loyalty and love, worry about reactions to social situations, sensitivity to abuse and rejection and negating the self to get sympathy.

The behaviors of anxious avoidant persons include avoiding people but experiencing loss of self-esteem; building up the self in a defensive way; struggling to maintain a sense of self-worth; a lack of insight; maintaining an unrealistic positive view of self; limited awareness of negative characteristics; unrealistic positive response to threats including separation, self-praise and denial of weakness, uncertainty of positive self-views and dismissal of positive feedback. The behaviors of persons with a disorganized attachment style may present problems with adaptation and social functioning that cannot be successfully managed without mental health intervention.

One may observe some of these behaviors in the self. If so, one needs to recognize that behavior can change. One needs to realize that negative feelings stored in the emotional center of the brain are seeking expression and controlling behavior. Using spiritual power to think about the reality of these feelings for the purpose of correcting original erroneous assumptions is required. For example, adults who did not become successfully attached to a primary attachment figure often assumed as children that the reason was because something was defective in them. They developed an insecure attachment style that has affected their interpersonal relationships into adulthood.

Spiritual power can be instrumental in rethinking and relearning feelings about indifference, neglect and rejection. This power is the ability to recognize and use the eternal dimension of the soul that also is the mind to correct mistaken assumptions that followed. Clear analytical thinking can resolve psychosocial problems.

God or Supreme Being may be an attachment figure for some individuals. They could be people who have an insecure attachment style who, through new experience with prayer and a faith based relationship with God, develop new neural pathways that promote a secure attachment style. This attachment is significant as positive ideas about self and others may arise with a sense of a positive relationship with God. This suggests that individuals who see God as a secure base would find that relationship helpful in seeking a solution to an emotional problem.

Self-worth is a concept related to spiritual power. Self-worth is a sense of one's intrinsic value. When one realizes that the spiritual power with which they have been endowed at birth by God or Supreme Being it naturally follows that nothing created by an eternal being can be bad in its nature. Created beings sometimes do bad things because free will exists but humanity is basically good.

There are some individuals who will not be able to use spiritual power to find solutions to emotional problems. Those persons who are unable to think clearly because of intellectual limitations or serious mental illness will find it difficult.

In summary, it is suggested that everyone realize the natural gift of spiritual power.

Realizing its availability and using it can make a difference in how one reacts to challenges. This power, because of its analytical property, provides a means of examining the reality of interpersonal and social experience in a way that can produce a new perspective. This new perspective can lead to freedom from anxiousness and a more satisfying life.

Chapter 5
A Process for Thinking

The principal idea of this book has been you are what you feel, but if you *think* it can get better. This chapter describes a process for thinking that may be useful to readers.

Clear productive thinking involves a review of those emotionally charged events in life from which erroneous assumptions were made about the self and others. A person can learn skills to set apart the damaged inner child from the potentially normal adult leading to increased self-awareness and improved social functioning. Being born into a dysfunctional family can contribute to emotional problems although this isn't necessarily true. Some members of the family may behave non-normatively, but if the primary attachment figure exhibits a secure attachment style and any one of her children was able to attach to her, that child may be strengthened by adversities and escape developing emotional problems later. Another factor is the amount of energy with which a child is endowed at conception. Those persons endowed with greater energy have a better chance of solving emotional problems before they become a problem. Similarly more intelligent persons are able to think through adverse experiences more effectively with less negative impact.

This thinking process will be explained clearly enough for a reader to be able to use it to solve emotional distress. There are three parts: context, explanation and thinking. The first step is to explore the context of the emotional problem. *Context* is a review of the developmental history of negative emotional experiences of indifference, neglect, rejection and traumatic events, as these are the main contributors to emotional problems. Context provides a clearer picture of strengths and weaknesses in adaptation and social functioning. Achieving this level of understanding can itself bring considerable relief from distress. Knowledge of context enables a person to begin to formulate a self-assessment of personality established through developmental history and the social environment in which the problem developed. Knowledge of these factors will result in a more objective perspective in which the context can be viewed as a causative agent rather than blaming the self.

Knowledge about context provides clarification of the circumstances surrounding the problem and what developmental and environmental factors have contributed to it. This will require some research of memory and reflection on the assumptions and feelings about the self. Concentrating on relationships with mother, father, brothers and sisters is necessary as these attachments are the ones through which self-esteem and feelings of self-worth were formed. A list of these events may be helpful in explanation, the next phase of the *thinking* process. Referring to Chapter 7 on attachment before beginning the explanation phase may provide a foundation for remembering significant emotional events that contributed to later emotional distress.

Explanation is a search for understanding the impact of negative and traumatic developmental events on attachment style remembered during the context phase. One will learn what assumptions and feelings about them were erroneous and need to be reframed and rethought in ways that change self-perception and attachment style. This thoughtful analysis can lead to increased self-awareness and takes both time and reflection. Remember feelings are never right or wrong or good or bad. Avoid judgments about yourself and others and their feelings and behaviors.

The next phase is *thinking*, a thoughtful consideration of explanation. The objective is a realization that paying attention to assumptions and feelings arising from developmental events are at the core of emotional distress. If one thinks clearly about what was learned about the self during the explanation phase, one will see the erroneous assumptions and feelings that have been in control of behavior. Thinking about how a negative core self-belief formed neural pathways that led to negative interpretations of self in social situations and interfered with adaptation and social functioning can aid in developing a positive perspective and improved problem solving.

Many people do not distinguish between thinking and feeling. *Thinking* is the action of using your mind to produce ideas, decisions, memories, etc. It generally is rational and purposeful.

Feeling is an emotional state or reaction that may be irrational. The principal behavioral change that is sought is to correct those behaviors characteristic of an insecure attachment style. This requires self-examination and thinking about feelings that resulted from some level of indifference, neglect or rejection by attachment figures during child and adolescent developmental periods. In many instances trauma such as physical or sexual abuse may have been part of the context. Neuroscience research results are that feelings that follow negative emotional experiences are stored in the emotional center of the brain. These feelings seek consciousness and are a primary source of emotional distress.

Thinking is a review of those incidents that were directly related to indifference, neglect or rejection by the primary caretaker, family or significant others that resulted in an insecure attachment style. The effect of trauma also needs to be remembered. It is the feelings that are the focus of attention. Children and adolescents who have strained relationships with primary attachment figures do not blame them for the feelings or the behavior as they realize that would create more conflict and more distress. Instead they make an assumption of self-blame. This results in believing they are bad which generates considerable guilt. Frequently, this guilt leads to self-punishing behavior such as choosing associates that are troublemakers or marrying a partner that also has a negative sense about self that makes the relationship very difficult and sometimes impossible in which to engage.

Remember you are what you feel but if you *think* it can get better. Thinking means looking at things realistically. The question of whether a person really is bad has to be answered.

It may be difficult but one must realize that the reality is that whatever negative experience occurred was not the fault of the individual. It is something that was done to them and not done by them. Therefore, the individual is not bad and does not need to feel guilty. Rethinking and relearning to determine the actual facts will provide a new and positive perspective. Searching for the truth can make a difference.

For review, there are three parts to this thinking process, context, explanation and thinking. *Context* consists of a review of the negative emotional events of indifference, neglect or rejection during developmental years. *Explanation* is seeking reasons for negative feelings that resulted from negative emotional events with significant others for which one was not at fault. *Thinking* is reflecting on an explanation of feelings about these events to relearn an appropriate response. Thinking clarifies detail. It is a rational look at the reality of circumstances. Thinking can help the individual to not hand over the judgment of one's value or worth to anyone, and to examine one's strengths or the things that are done well. Thinking can help to not take corrective suggestions as criticism or take others' negative remarks personally. Instead, ask them, or think, why would they say or do something negative? What is their problem? Engaging fully in this process can have the effect of correcting erroneous feelings and relief from anxiousness. This process can be used effectively by most people.

Chapter 6
Self-education for Self-intervention

The purpose of this chapter is to further encourage self-education for self-intervention through the use of a process for thinking. The content is a social work theory based approach to Explanation and Thinking, the second and third phases of the process. Knowledge of theory is empowering. It encourages self-confidence in problem solving and provides a tool for thinking about emotions that is part of self-education.

A self-education process consisting of ideas from Attachment Theory, the subject of Chapter 8, and Cognitive Theory supplemented by constructivism and Vygotsky's Sociocultural Theory were described in sufficient detail for those readers seeking a self-help guide to mental health. Critical thinking about this combination of ideas organizes self- intervention. Ideas extracted from Cognitive Theory are methods leading to understanding the implications of Attachment Theory as applied to the self. Vygotsky's sociocultural theory and Constructivist Theory broadens this understanding.

A major element in self-intervention is awareness of how feeling and behavior are based on learning from the experiences of childhood and adolescence. Some individuals refer to this as insight that results from a release from repression of emotionally charged memories. Another way of looking at this is that it is the recovery of memories from the preconscious mind that enables rethinking and relearning of erroneous assumptions made about negative emotional experiences. In either case awareness or insight as explanation is necessary.

People who are anxious or depressed or both want explanations for their difficult feelings. They have not learned that feelings are just feelings that are never good or bad or right or wrong. They have not learned about the internalization of a negative self and feelings of self-blame resulting from indifference, neglect or rejection by attachment figures, peers, fellow workers or others with whom they have a meaningful relationship. They become anxious about themselves and suspicious of others. These feelings affect adaptation and social functioning. For this chapter adaptation is defined as successful management of drives, impulses and instincts and social functioning as behavior acceptable to observers.

Much information about theories of assessment and treatment of emotional distress is available on the Internet or in college libraries. Suffice it to say that any person seeking self-education must have sufficient knowledge to effectively use at least one theory.

Attachment Theory was selected for application of concepts in this chapter. A child's attachment to the primary attachment figure, usually the mother, and secondary attachment figures, usually the father and siblings is the foundation for normative emotional development. When attachment is successful a child will adopt a secure attachment style. When attachment is unsuccessful the child may adopt one of three insecure attachment styles, anxious avoidant, anxious ambivalent or disorganized.

Some behaviors of insecure attachment styles are presented in Chapter 8 on Attachment Theory. For the purpose of review behaviors of the anxious ambivalent and anxious avoidant styles are mentioned here. For the anxious ambivalent style they include: confusion about approaching or avoiding others; strong emphasis on getting attention; continuously and compulsively seeking affection and emotional support; intense fear of rejection; doubts about being able to obtain loyalty and love; worry about reactions to social situations; vulnerability to abuse and rejection; self-focused attention; and devaluation of self to get sympathy from others. For the anxious avoidant style they are: diminished self-esteem; defensive self-enhancement; a struggle to maintain a sense of self-worth; lack of insight; unrealistic positive view of self; limited awareness of negative characteristics; unrealistic positive response to the threat of separation; self-praise and denial of weakness; uncertainty of positive self-views and dismissal of positive feedback. For the disorganized style they are: no strategy to deal with unpredictable parents; considerable fear; unresolved trauma; inability to self-soothe and serious psychiatric problems such as borderline personality disorder (BPD); pervasive instability in moods, interpersonal relationships, self image and behavior.

Self-education may help to establish a new view of self and others so emotional distress is relieved and behaviors become more normal. This often occurs when one learns that the assumptions of self-blame for the indifference, neglect or rejection experienced from attachment figures were erroneous.

Cognitive theory was developed by Aaron Beck. It is a prominent intervention theory that focuses on problem solving by changing thinking. Beck was a psychoanalyst whose experience led him to discover that helping a person to think realistically about feelings following emotionally distressing events was more effective than other methods. Albert Ellis is another cognitive theorist who proposed that it isn't distressful events that bother us but what our reaction is to them. Children and adolescents often blame themselves for problems with parents or significant others with whom they have a close relationship. This usually results in negating self and subsequent difficulties in interpersonal relationships Cognitive Theory provides a way to rethink and relearn responses to distressing events.

This can lead to correcting erroneous perceptions of self-blame and a negative self. Flawed perceptions lead to false interpretations that sooner or later will result in emotional distress. One can self-teach the *thinking* process described in Chapter 5 to learn more. Thinking correctly about emotionally charged events may lead to constructing a realistic meaning about what happened. This new perception may relieve anxiousness and a depressed mood.

Lev S. Vygotsky founded sociocultural theory, also known as Social Development Theory. He was a Russian psychologist who made significant contributions to education and psychology. Vygotsky was concerned about development of the self and how problems in development may create emotional distress. Learning about life as a development of self or becoming what you are may be very helpful to those experiencing emotional distress Vygotsky's theory may be described as relational as he believed that learning occurs through inputs from the culture and social environment, especially close interpersonal relationships. He rejected the idea of a separation between learning and development, instead believing that learning leads to development. Development is the social activity of becoming what you are to be.

Vygotsky believed that development was enhanced by learning through interaction with others, that learning is not development but that mental development would be impossible apart from learning. Thus learning is a necessary process of developing psychological functions, i.e. feeling and thinking.

Vygotsky's ideas about learning may be applied to self-education. One can engage in a self-educational process of relearning and rethinking erroneous feeling responses to perceived negative emotional experiences that occurred primarily during developmental years. What was learned through negative experiences affected becoming in a problem direction. When self-education results in understanding emotional distress, a reevaluation of perception and response will occur and becoming, or development, proceeds normatively.

Vygotsky introduced the Zone of Proximal Development (ZPD) related to learning. This zone is where the interaction with others aids the process of becoming. Vygotsky proposed that there are two levels of development, actual and potential. Actual development is what one is able to accomplish alone in resolving emotional distress. Potential development is what one can accomplish with the assistance of a therapist.

Critical thinking, discussed in Chapter 7, increases a person's ability to think rationally and realistically. Critical thinking breaks the connection between feeling and behavior. One must be motivated and willing to engage in critical thinking if it to be successful. Critical thinking skills and activities are: analyzing the emotional problem by answering the questions who, what, where, why and how; use of mental health theory such as Attachment Theory that is suggested herein to make a self-assessment by examining strengths and weaknesses in your developmental history related to the emotional problem and its resolution; synthesizing the answers to the previous questions to begin self-intervention; reasoning about where to begin problem solving; identifying behaviors that demonstrate success in resolving the problem; and finally, evaluating the process to determine its success.

Constructivism Theory fits Vygotsky's theory of development or becoming as it is a theory that humans construct their own reality. However, that perception of reality may not always be valid. Vygotsky's concept of development or becoming what you are to be in your life is central to his ideas. When one thinks about the process of becoming objectives and goals will develop and become a guide for self-education.

Knowledge of neuroscience research findings, especially about neural pathways, is related to Vygotsky's concept of becoming. Emotional experience, both positive and negative, generates neural pathways that are stored in the emotional center of the brain. These stored memories continuously seek expression in behavior. The negative memories may prompt behavior that is symptomatic of conflict. These negative memories may be replaced by positive memories of new experiences of similar events. New corrective emotional experience generates new neural pathways that replace the old conflicted ones and feelings and behavior will change to a normative type. Neural pathways because they become part of the brain are part of anatomy. This suggests that emotional distress has a physical base rather than emotional. For some people this will be a game changer as a physical problem is easier to understand than an emotional one.

This chapter was about self-education for intervention in emotional distress. The rationale is that the suggested combination of theories provides a way to reflect on the pathways of development of emotional distress. People who are anxious or depressed are looking for explanations for their distress. Combining Attachment Theory and Cognitive Theory with Constructivism Theory in Vygotsky's Sociocultural Theory is way to self-educate to find explanations.

The process is not as complicated as it appears. In brief what is involved is learning the basics of the theories discussed in this chapter and doing more study about them if necessary, recalling feelings of attachment one had with family or significant others, realizing how much culture and environment impact a person's sense of self and others, understanding errors made in interpreting the meaning of emotional or traumatic events, reflective thinking, using some techniques in Motivational Interviewing, to analyze the meaning of troubling events in your life and making a plan for change based on the results.

Motivational Interviewing (MI) is a counseling technique developed by clinical psychologists William R. Miller and Stephen Rollnick. It is a directive counseling style for behavior change that helps clients explore and resolve ambivalence. It has four parts:

open-ended questions, affirmation, reflection and summary (OARS). Open-ended questions require a narrative response about a person's experiences, perspectives, and ideas. The questions guide the client to reflection change. Affirmation of strengths and past successes build a person's confidence in their ability to change. Reflections are based on careful listening and trying to understand what the person is saying, by repeating, rephrasing or offering a deeper guess about what the person is trying to communicate. Summarizing ensures shared understanding and reinforces key points.

MI is a technique used by mental health professionals but it can be adapted to self-use. To begin ask yourself what are the exact facts of the distressing emotional experience as you can recall them. This will take some time. Write them down. As you proceed affirm your skills in seeking and clarifying facts as the basis for distress. Think of similar problem situations experienced in the past and the successful problem solving you accomplished then. Reflect on what deeper feelings emerge in your mind as you think about the written facts This will take time Don't hurry. The thinking process will consolidate ideas. A summary of your analysis will lead to decision making about what to do to solve the problem.

The content of the chapter is recommended as a way of self-education for intervention in emotional distress. One may need some help from a mental health professional but self-education will enhance that contact.

Chapter 7
Critical Thinking for Self-awareness

The theme of this book has been *thinking*. This chapter seeks to clarify further what this means. Almost everyone has the ability to use critical thinking to reflect on experiences and the feelings associated with them. Many people have a difficult emotional start in life and there are a variety of reasons why children are treated indifferently, neglected or rejected. Mothers may have become pregnant before they were ready. Marriage relationships may not have established sufficient solidarity to withstand the introduction of a third person. Economic circumstances may have been difficult enough because one of the partners had to quit working or lost a job for other reasons. Having a child significantly increases a couple's responsibility for which one or both persons may not have been ready. There are many situations that can generate negative feelings toward a child or children. Often children feel distressed neglected or unloved. These feelings are stored in the emotional center of the brain. They promote anxiousness about the self and others that interferes with adaptation and social functioning. For some persons these troubling memories may be so disturbing as to result in emotional distress. The question is what can these individuals do to help themselves? Critical thinking will help relearn erroneous responses to these events. Critical thinking is one extension of ideas in the previous chapter about self-education.

There are several skills and activities required for critical thinking. First, one must be fully ready and willing to think about life's experiences and what one has learned from them. Second, one has to be aware of logic that may be defined as valid reasoning. Validity may be thought to be truth or fact. Critical thinking is reflecting on what was learned from experience and deciding whether what was learned was a truthful or factual result of an experience. Third, one has to develop some skill in reflective awareness and logical reasoning. This means one has to have the ability to recall details of indifferent, neglectful or rejecting experiences. These may have occurred with a parent or parents or peers or another person with whom one had a close relationship. One must be able to recall feelings about the self or about others that were related to the negative experience. Remembering feelings, because they may have been threatening, can be difficult to recall for some individuals. Talking with a trusted friend or relative who has realistic knowledge of the problematic emotional events may be helpful. Sometimes professional assistance may be required.

Critical thinking skill is not something everyone has. However, it can be learned and with practice can become helpful. The traditional questions of *who, what, where, when, why and how* are a place to begin. Who was involved? What happened that generated the anxious memory? Where did it occur? When during the developmental years did this experience happen? Why is whatever happened having such an emotional effect? How is this affecting social functioning?

Answering all these questions can take time so one should not be impatient. One needs to give permission to the self to remember. Writing notes about what is remembered can be helpful as a future reference. After the process of answering the questions, the next step is to put the details of the information into a way of relating the answers to the individual questions that results in a clear perspective of what really happened and what were the outcomes. Then one has to evaluate the significance of the event and whether the outcomes were realistic.

Everyone has an attachment behavior system (ABS) that is activated when there is a threat of separation from the attachment figure, whether physical or emotional. If the attachment figure is not nearby or is unresponsive the attached person will display anxious behaviors that continue until the attachment figure returns and pays attention to the child or adult. Feelings about these separation events are stored in the emotional center of the brain and often are the cause of emotional distress because they may lead to an insecure attachment style. Critical thinking about attachment style is the activity of the third phase of the thinking process presented in Chapter 5. It will clarify the impact of developmental factors explored in context or how developmental and environmental factors are the background for the emotional problems that a person is experiencing as the result.

An example is a male, only child with parents who did not relate well to each other.

Mother worked full time and returned to work two weeks after giving birth. Father was a farmer whose work was outside. This answers the "who" question. The baby was left alone much of the time in the house that often was cold because the coal furnace needed continuous stoking. That answers both the "what" and "where" questions. An additional fact of where is that there were no families with children in the neighborhood until a family with four children moved into a house about a half mile away. Until then the child had no playmates and was alone most of the time. Being alone and without significant attachment to either parent during early development years answers the "when" question.

Answers to the why and how questions provide information about the emotional effect. The child did not receive the needed attention. As consciousness developed anxiousness came with it. The child wet the bed and frequently had very painful stomach aches during the night. At age eight when the family moved nearby he found a friend but frequently was unsure of the sincerity of the friendship. No one ever came to his house to ask him to play. He wondered why that was. He attended a religion based school in a nearby city and stayed at his aunt's house after school where he met a new friend. There were other children in the neighborhood but none of them became close friends. Here too no one ever came to call for him to play. During elementary school years his mother was asked to come to the school to talk about his behavior. It was never explained why this occurred and no suggestions about behavior change were ever provided. The same behavior of others not seeking him occurred through high school. He had several acquaintances and spent time with many of them but did not have a close relationship except with a girlfriend he dated steadily during the last two years of high school. He attended a university in a distant city and that relationship terminated as she wanted to get married. He didn't get along very well with his roommates during his first and second years. He met another student during the second half of the sophomore year and lived with him during his junior year. That person changed majors and dropped back a year so that friendship was lost. During his senior year he was assigned a new roommate that had a different major and many established friendships. That relationship didn't go well. He always felt socially anxious and lonely at the university. At the end of the sophomore year he met a girl at a local dance with whom he quickly developed a close relationship. He spent a lot of time with her during the summer. When he returned to the university she wrote him a letter every day. This expression of friendliness was a great relief. It was easier to withstand the perceived unfriendliness at the university as there always was something good coming. This relationship continued and a year after graduation they were married.

It is apparent that this individual was affected by his experiences during his developmental years. He internalized a negative sense of himself that continuously interfered with successful adaptation and social functioning. Fortunately he chose to study for an advanced degree in a helping profession. This experience was very difficult but also quite helpful as he learned about himself and his emotional weaknesses. His wife became a nurse during their courtship. She was exceptionally helpful and emotionally supportive. She became his primary attachment figure. Through her clarification of his many negative thoughts she contributed to his realistic thinking about his parents and his interpersonal problems. Through education he learned critical thinking skills so this combination made a significant difference in his self-assessment. Although he continued to be anxious it did not reach a level where it interfered with adaptation and social functioning.

What exactly did this individual do that was helpful in decreasing anxiousness? Two general activities were involved: education and marriage. The curriculum of the helping profession focused on self-awareness as part of preparation for dealing with persons that have emotional problems. The internship part of the program was especially worthwhile as the relationship with the supervisor was excellent and provided even more self-understanding. Marriage also provided an advantage. His wife became aware of the sources of his anxiousness and helped him sort out feelings about his developmental years. As she got to know his parents she realized how their personalities and their relationship affected her husband. She also was a professional and had gained many insights that she used to clarify his self-understanding.

Through talking with his wife he was able to use critical thinking skills to analyze the impact of the negative emotional events of his life and synthesize these ideas into a new framework

There are many individuals who have had similar experiences. This brief narrative depicts an example of problems occurring during development years and what happens to a person's self image as a result. However, rethinking the circumstances can bring a person to an awareness of not being at fault and therefore changing self-perception and finding a secure attachment style.

Most psychosocial problems involve distressed feelings about the self and others.

A definition of feelings is that they are an emotional state or reaction, a response to external or internal stimuli. Sometimes feelings are irrational. Rational feelings have a reality base. Irrational feelings often arise from internalized negative emotional experiences. A rational emotional response occurs following an interpretation of a behavior. Someone you respect compliments you about doing something well and you feel gratified. The opposite is true when someone tells you something negative about yourself. You feel criticized and may get angry and make an erroneous irrational feeling assumption about yourself and others that is stored in the emotional center of the brain.

As behavior is influenced by one's feelings and thoughts, thinking about differences between them and how each effect life's decisions is one way to change inappropriate behavior. Most persons who have emotional problems also have a history of trauma especially characterized by indifference, neglect and rejection in the early developmental years and sometimes during adolescence when self-identity is formed. Thinking rationally about feelings also may generate a realization that whatever problematic feelings one has, even those that are the most negative, resentful or harmful, are normative because they are the outcome of the experiences.

Some knowledge about neuroscience may help critical thinking as well. Many adults have memories of negative and rejecting experiences with one parent or both. A common reaction for developing children is to wonder what's wrong with them that caused the parents to react negatively or to reject them. This negative self-assessment generates a reaction that contributes to an insecure attachment style that is reactivated repeatedly in other relationships.

These experiences form neural pathways in the brain where they will influence behavior and feelings. Critical thinking about these experiences can result in developing new neural pathways that replace the negative pathways. This change may result in problem resolution and improved adaptation and social functioning. Neuroscience findings, especially about neural pathways and neural plasticity, highlight the contributions of physiology to the assessment and management of emotional disorders.

Neuroscience also produced evidence of neural plasticity that may underlie the brain's ability to adapt and change in response to the environment. Neural plasticity is the ability of the brain to form new neural connections throughout life. New positive neuronal pathways are formed in response to new situations or to positive changes in relationships or environment that replace the old negative ones. This can improve adaptation and social functioning.

Chapter 8
Attachment Theory

This chapter describes Attachment Theory. It was chosen for emphasis in this book as it is a theory that can be very helpful when using the thinking process described in Chapter 5.

John Bowlby M.D., founder of attachment theory, wrote a report for the World Health Organization entitled *Maternal Care and Mental Health*. This report contributed substantially to understanding the concepts of mental health and mental ill-health. In this monograph, Bowlby made it very clear that deprivation of the mother-child relationship, depending upon the length and type, contributed to psychopathology. His work with children at London's Tavistock clinic, along with the research evidence presented by other psychiatrists and mental health workers around the world, made clear that the attachment of the child to the mother or permanent mother substitute was essential to mental health. Bowlby has written extensively on the subject of separation and loss of the primary caretaker. This loss has a seriously negative effect on mental health, interpersonal relationships and social functioning of the child involved. It is reasonable to conclude, based upon the evidence, that there is a relationship between health and mental health and attachment theory. This idea has led to an understanding that persons with mental health problems are likely to experience physical health issues as well.

Attachment theory is significant in understanding emotions and behavior. It concerns the relationship between the child and the primary caretaker which, in our culture, is usually the mother. Close attachment to the primary caretaker contributes to the formation of an attachment bond that can affect the individual's level of adaptation and social functioning throughout life. Attachment also affects the relationship between adults.

Problems with attachment may be noticed in a child's reaction when the primary attachment figure leaves the child's sight.

Immediate signs of distress may appear including crying which is a frequent response. When the attachment figure returns the child is quieted and the distress disappears. Another example can be seen in the "peek-a-boo" game. Notice the child's happy response when sight of the attachment figure is restored.

Reflect on what type of relationship you had with your mother. Was she available and sensitive to your needs as you expressed them? Was she emotionally supportive? Was she critical of you? Was she consistent in what she said and how did that affect you? Was she frightening or confusing in her responses to you? The behaviors and thoughts coming from her had a lot to do with forming the attachment style you have today. You can change it if it isn't working, but first you need to understand what it is and not to make a critical judgment about it. Of course if it's a secure style then you're not having very many problems. If it's an insecure style you may wish to change it because it may not be leading to the level of satisfaction you desire.

Bowlby also described an attachment behavioral system. This system is activated when there is a threat of separation from the attachment figure whether real or emotional. Physical separation is easy to understand and may happen if either child or mother stays in the hospital after the other is discharged. It may occur if the primary attachment figure leaves on a long vacation when the child is very young. Generally, these separations do not have a serious effect unless the separation is lengthy or the attitude of the mother was such that the birth was not a welcome event in the mother's life or in the family's expectations. These feelings sometimes can lead to continuing difficulties of acceptance which will establish a barrier in the attachment relationship. Other barriers to bonding and attachment, such as when a caretaker is indifferent, neglectful or rejecting, may have the same effect. In such cases the attachment system organizes an adaptive response aimed at restoring the availability of the attachment figure. When the attachment figure returns the attachment system is deactivated although there can be some residual anxiousness. A failure of restoration contributes to anxiety.

Emotional separation also may have an effect on the developing child. This occurs when there is indifference, neglect or rejection by the primary attachment figure and is often more difficult for a child to comprehend. There is the potential for the development of dysfunctional attitudes and behaviors that may have a long term effect and may require the intervention of a mental health professional.

There are three other points that should be made here. Ontogenetic endowment may be a factor in how a child reacts to separation. These are characteristics that come with conception. It isn't well understood, but for whatever reason, some children are not significantly negatively affected by separations from the primary attachment figure. There is a quality in their genetic makeup that helps defeat the negative effect, and some children may become emotionally stronger as the result. Separations that occur a few years after birth also may not result in anxiousness when the early years of the child-mother relationship were unusually positive. In this case, the child develops such a positive sense of self that such an untoward event of separation has little or no effect.

The second point relates to the adoption of a child. If the adoption occurs shortly after birth and a normal attachment bond develops between the child and the adoptive mother the chances of a problem emotional effect is decreased. Here, ontogenetic endowment also may make a difference.

The third point is about a child born under circumstances where placement in foster care is necessary. The effect can be problematic. This separation may create anxiousness although the innate need of the child to attach may be partially fulfilled by the foster mother. A child placed in multiple foster homes may develop a lasting feeling of anxiousness and abandonment.

Lack of attachment can increase feelings of guilt. It can also generate angry feelings that include resentment at not being adequately nurtured. This combination often provokes suspiciousness about others. When attachment to the primary caretaker is missing, how can it be expected that the child will be able to form positive and lasting relationships with other human beings? This pattern can continue into adulthood if nothing is done to change it. The process can perpetuate itself as mothers and fathers who feel inadequate tend to relate to their children in ways that promote similar feelings in them. This may continue until something happens to break the cycle.

One group of attachment theorists believe there are four types of attachment: secure, dismissive, preoccupied and fearful. Another group believes that the types are secure and insecure with three subtypes: anxious avoidant, anxious ambivalent and disorganized. These types correspond with each other in terms of reaction and can be described in the same way.

The type of style the individual develops is generally based upon the response of the attachment figure, usually the mother, although the family system may be a contributing element. These styles are significant in that they take a while to develop during early childhood but stabilize and continue through adolescence and adulthood. Everyone has an attachment style. It is important to think about the attachment style you have and its affect on your relationships with everyone including your associates at work, your personal life and even your relationship with casual acquaintances.

Children who have experienced the consistent availability and positive response of an attachment figure have a secure type of attachment that is a positive view of the self and others. A secure attachment style is established by a secure base provided by the primary attachment figure that actively cares for a child or the other in an adult relationship. This positive view of the self generates confidence and improves a person's ability to be comfortable in maintaining attachment relationships even when those figures are not readily available. It also engenders a feeling of being cared for by others. In this parenting style, the child feels safe and protected and learns self-soothing. A consistent caring response from attachment figured, especially the primary, results in the development of an attachment bond which is the basis for developing attachments to others. A child with a secure attachment bond feels confident about social relationships with a sense of strength or self-esteem that is characteristic. It is easy for them to make friends and they have a more objective perception of others. They have confidence in interpersonal relationships and are not afraid to take reasonable chances. Their adaptation skills are developed and their social functioning is within normal limits. This secure child is likely to become a secure adult who has the capacity for effective parenting.

Insecure attachment styles are characterized by negative working models in which a person experiences decreased self-esteem and self-confidence and a lack of trust in relationships with others. This is complicated by the view that others are not caring and responsive. The *anxious avoidant attachment style* is characterized by a positive view of the self but a negative view of others. They prefer not to have emotional closeness with others and make more of their accomplishments than is realistic. They often are narcissistic and fantasize about being powerful. They deny vulnerability and pretend self-sufficiency. They avoid seeking out an attachment figure. They prefer self-sufficiency without depending on others or having others depend on them. In this example, the caretaker is generally critical and dismissive. This attachment style extends into adulthood with all the avoidant characteristics.

The person who has an *anxious ambivalent attachment style* has a negative view of self and a positive view of others. They want to be close to the caregiver all the time and become very upset when he/she is absent. They strive for emotional intimacy with others and are uncomfortable without close relationships. They have a high need for dependency, are typically quite anxious and experience fear of abandonment and rejection. Their self-esteem is low. They tend to internalize the anxiousness of the caretaker who is inconsistent in her response. Anxious ambivalent children will likely mature as anxious ambivalent adults with corresponding emotional problems.

The *disorganized attachment style* is characterized by a negative view of both self and others. Developing trusting relationships is difficult because they fear close relationships although they have a strong need for them. There are conflicting feelings with many ups and down\s and the caretaker is both frightening and confusing. Disorganized children continue to be disorganized as adults. This style often requires mental health intervention.

Bowlby developed the concept of internal working models, or mental representations, that are a set of expectations and beliefs about the self and others. If a child is feeling bad and receives a prompt response from a loving adult who makes her/him feel better, she/he will learn that her/his behaviors are linked with the positive behaviors of a caregiver. Then a feeling of deserving of being loved and nurtured can occur and a more generalized view that others are likely to be there to help and protect also develops. These are characteristics of a secure attachment style. On the other hand a negative or uncaring response from a caretaker can lead to an internal working model of the attachment figure as being rejecting.

This can lead to a feeling of being unworthy of care and that others cannot be expected to provide help and support. This type of working model is associated with an insecure attachment style.

Bowlby observed that these all of these models are established within the first few years of life and as children get older they become increasingly resistant to change. Children's behaviors become organized around expectations of themselves and others and in time that will influence how others relate to them. Positive and negative cycles of reinforcement follow. Persons who feel good about themselves and expect others to respond positively will present themselves to others in a way that suggests trust. On the other hand those who expect rejection and have low self esteem send messages distancing themselves from others. This can result in withdrawal of others and a negative feedback loop of perceived rejection.

Individuals who have caretakers with whom they were not adequately attached tend to seek out other individuals who have had similar developmental experiences. The old saying "Birds of a feather flock together" has a lot of truth in it. These individuals tend to seek others like them for marital partners so it is not a wonder these marriages don't work. Still the needs are so strong these couples tend to stay together. That also is true regarding those chosen as friends.

These feelings are all the result of lack of attachment or come from internalizing negative messages. They are a normal aftermath of what was learned. They don't work and there is a feeling of discomfort. If you are experiencing these feelings, know that they are not your fault. However, that doesn't mean you don't have a responsibility to do something about them.

If you are a parent and you are aware of having a problem attachment style you will want to reflect on what is happening within your marital relationship and with your children's behavior. Being conscious of the problem has the potential of creating a focus on change that can be corrective. The singular corrective action is to develop and display a caring, engaged, interested and supportive behavior style. This requires insight into yourself and your developmental experiences. Recalling some of these memories may be emotionally painful but calling them to consciousness can be helpful in the long run. Seeking professional help may also be necessary. You may also want to be aware of the strengths and weaknesses of those whom your children choose as friends. Get to know them as well as you can and get to know their parents too.

When a person has an attachment figure that has either an anxious avoidant, anxious ambivalent or disorganized attachment style, difficulties with adaptation and social functioning are likely to develop. If you happen to be one of those persons, you have an explanation about some of your feelings. You will realize the reason for the emotional distance you feel from your primary attachment figure and possibly from secondary figures and others with whom you have a personal relationship. You will realize the reason for the self-conscious and anxious feelings about yourself. If you have an uneasy feeling of suspiciousness about how others feel about you, the reasons for that will become clearer. You may want to consult a mental health professional.

It makes sense that finding a caring relationship can make a difference in your feelings. However, be cautious in this search as individuals who have an anxious avoidant, anxious ambivalent or disorganized attachment style tend to choose relationships with others who have the same style.

As with other relationships, marital relationships are often affected by the attachment styles of the partners. An individual that has experienced indifference, neglect or rejection brings into the marital relationship the frustrations and self-concerns related to the negative experiences. How these issues are managed will affect the marriage. Often it will be necessary for both to visit with a marriage counselor who knows attachment theory so both can better understand the source of their conflict and begin to take corrective action.

The behaviors associated with the two most common insecure styles are listed below. Fortunately, the secure style is the most frequently observed. However, among those persons who are experiencing emotional distress or mental illness, insecure styles are observed more frequently. The reader may examine these insecure style behaviors to learn whether any are part of their style. The presence of at least some of the characteristics can mean that one has an insecure attachment style. However, since any one of them may affect the capacity for adaptation and social function, some behavioral change may be necessary. Such change usually can be made by thinking about the effect of inappropriate behavior on others.

It may be helpful for some readers to list a few of the behaviors of the anxious ambivalent and anxious avoidant attachment styles. For the *anxious ambivalent style* they are: expecting partners to meet needs for affection, feeling unsure about how to engage with others, emphasis on getting attention, fear of rejection, constantly looking for affection and support, worry about how to react in social situations and concern about being abused or rejected. For the *anxious avoidant style* they are: difficulty sustaining feelings of self-worth, absence of insight, responding in an unrealistic way to threats such as separation and loss of a significant relationship, little ability to see negative characteristics in the self and promoting an unrealistic positive view of self.

The conclusion of some after reading this chapter may be an awareness of having developed an insecure attachment style. When such a style develops at an early age it usually extends into adolescence and adulthood. However, styles can change. Finding a new positive attachment from which a secure style may be achieved is possible through developing new relationships such as marriage or attachment to a significant other. Sometimes a good approach is to seek mental health counseling as a provider may become an attachment figure.

Chapter 9
Individual Self-worth

This chapter is about individual self-worth, its significance in adaptation and social functioning and some suggestions about maintaining and increasing it. The content also will help in the use of the thinking process as described in Chapter 5.

Self-worth is a sense of one's own value. There is a distinction between valuing one's self in terms of who you are and what you do. The more frequently asked question when first meeting others concerns what they do versus who they are. Every human has worth just because they are alive. Worth is an inherent quality in humanity. Every human is unique and different from every other human. Every human is a valued piece of the makeup of humanity.

Self-worth and self-esteem are often seen as equivalent terms. One potential problem with this is the tendency to measure self-esteem in comparison to others especially in the competitive culture in which we live. Self-esteem often is based on what a person does or what they have rather than on their intrinsic value as a human being.

Determining self-worth through external measures of comparison fails to bolster self-worth. There always will be somebody perceived to have a more important social position or more or better worldly goods. It is every individual's uniqueness that gives worth. Therefore it is important to examine one's strengths and potential for accomplishment as indications of self-worth and self-esteem.

Explanatory theories in psychology, such as those of Freud's psychoanalytic theory, Klein's object relations theory, Erikson's psychosocial theory and Bowlby's attachment theory, all propose that feelings, especially those that are formed during early developmental years, are major factors in adaptation, social functioning and self-worth. How one copes with drives, instincts and interpersonal relationships and behaves in ways that are accepted by observers contribute to feelings of self-worth.

Humans are a combination of a unique genetic makeup and what we learn as we develop, primarily from caretakers or attachment figures. Self-worth is established when perceptions of these relationships are positive and internalized. On the other hand, if these relationships are characterized by indifference, neglect or rejection it is likely that what will be internalized is a negative sense of self. This may generate inaccurate perceptions leading to assumptions or concepts about reality that are erroneous.

When a negative sense of self develops during early developmental years a child also may internalize a feeling of being bad because the blame for the indifferent, neglectful or rejecting parent is assumed to be self-generated. A child will not blame a parent, especially mother, out of fear that this will make things worse and because the thinking operation of the mind is not well enough developed to conceptualize reality.

This negative sense is stored in the brain, continues to seek expression and interferes with a feeling of self-worth. It often is accompanied by negative thoughts about the self that inhibit normative adaptation and social functioning. Managing the drives and instincts promoted by the unconscious mind and maintaining successful interpersonal relationships becomes more difficult. These problems generate more self-abasement and become a negative feedback loop that may lead to withdrawal from social contacts and suspiciousness about others.

It is the erroneous assumptions and resultant feelings that may lead to inappropriate behavior. If the assumption is that one is at fault for the indifferent, neglectful or rejecting attitude of attachment figures the burden of these feelings may become habitual. This can negate self-worth that is significant in maintaining positive mental health.

What can one do to maintain or restore self-worth and self-esteem? There are several ways that can contribute to this end. The main theme of this book is thinking about feelings and that is a place to begin. You may want to review the thinking process described in Chapter 5 and the concept of critical thinking described in Chapter 7. One needs to remember difficult events that occurred during developmental years. The feeling responses to these events and the assumptions that were made about them need to be recalled. Sometimes making a list may help. As the events and assumptions are recalled think about whether they were correct and fit reality. Were you really at fault for the indifferent, neglectful or rejecting behavior of a parent? Was your assumption of self-blame truly justified? What were the facts of the situation? One thing to look at closely is the developmental history of each of your parents. What was their relationship with their parents? Is there a history of substance abuse or emotional problems? Did your parents have a history of substance abuse or dysfunctional emotional responses and behavior? Do you have a history of being physically or emotionally abused? How did your parents relate to each other? Did your parents get a divorce when you were young? Was there a period of separation from your mother or family? Were you ever legally removed from your parents or placed in a foster home? These are some examples of questions that might aid in a review of experiences that decreased self-worth. The feelings of any one or a number of these experiences are stored in the brain and may be responsible for your self-critical inner voice and spontaneous negative self-thoughts.

Think realistically as an adult about these assumptions and feelings. Differentiate your adult thinking from your child feeling and develop a different perception of the experiences. This will promote a different and more realistic concept and likely free you from the guilt or shame that you may have felt. It is a way of improving and maintaining a sense of self-worth and self-esteem.

Another way of improving and maintaining a sense of self-worth and self-esteem is to stop comparing yourself to others Think of *your* uniqueness and *your* strengths and skills. Give yourself credit for these attributes. Focus on all the positives about yourself and your accomplishments. Forget and forgive yourself for the mistakes of the past.

Associate with others who share your beliefs and values. Help others whenever it is appropriate. Be kind to others and to yourself. Consider educating yourself professionally or technologically. If you are married and having problems, work to change and get professional help if necessary. Choose a vocation that fits your skills. Be proud of your work and the contribution you make. Remember that humanity needs a person to fill every work position and that your place in the scheme of things is an important square in the quilt of all the complex needs that must be met for the sake of advancing culture.

Religion is another way to achieve and maintain self-worth. Religiosity is significant in mental health and in maintaining overall coping mechanisms that contribute to successful adaptation and social functioning. The link between religious belief and a positive self-concept is real. It can be safely inferred that self-worth and self-esteem are integral parts of a positive self-concept.

It is reasonable that a belief in God or a Supreme Power, or whatever other title might be used by forms of religious belief, is necessary. For some people believing in God may be difficult because human senses are not capable of experiencing a spiritual entity. Therefore we are left with an intellectual approach or reasoning or simply faith to arrive at a concept about the existence of God.

You probably are familiar with the life and death cycle of all nature. Everything in nature, all humans and animals, come to life for some period of time and then die. If you think about it the question is: what generates this cycle and keeps it in order? Certainly no human, no matter how powerful, could do this. A part of this question also is: where did this begin and what or who started the cycle? No human could do this so it must be a being that is superhuman. It also logically has to be a being that has no beginning or end, an existence that can only be attributed to a spirit. This spirit is the first cause of anything that exists. This is the "first cause" argument for the existence of God proposed by Thomas Aquinas, a Greek philosopher and theologian. It is very logical. Can you come up with an argument against it?

One may argue that the foregoing is just intellectual. However, look at it from a practical point of view. Who could create a human with all its functions and potential about which there still are many unknowns? Who could create a tree, or landscape, or mountains, or streams or the availability of underground water? There must be a being that can do all this that many people call God.

One way to examine this further is to explore the connection between religious belief and Divine law, as expressed in the Ten Commandments of God, and a feeling of self-worth. It is safe to state that a feeling of self-worth is related to a sense of being a good person. One way to measure this sense of goodness is following a set of rules, such as the Ten Commandments that are accepted by many people in our culture. There is an aspect to the Commandments that can be quite comforting whether or not one believes in God. Many emotional and relationship problems arise from a lack of structure for behavior that the Commandments as rules can provide. The first three commandments refer to God but the last seven set limits on human behavior. They concern respect for parents, stealing, killing, false statements about others, adultery and taking another's goods or another's wife. All of these are serious transgressions that cover those behaviors that require rules that are part of structure. If one behaves following the Commandments it is reasonable to believe that behavior will be normative.

The Koran, the sacred book of Islam, has reference to Commandments. It is safe to state that this concept of rules for behavior is characteristic of most major religious belief systems.

Accepting the Commandments or the rules of other religious belief systems establishes a relationship with God or Allah or a Supreme Power. These rules place limitations on behavior in relationships with others. Following these rules as an accepted order of behavior will lead to acceptance and regard by others that promotes a feeling of self-worth.

Another possible way of increasing and sustaining self-worth is through prayer. Prayer is an individual matter. There are formal prayers in every religious belief system. There also are many informal prayers that are infrequently verbalized but silently expressed. Research about prayer and its effect on the brain has suggested definitely that prayer affects the brain in positive ways.

The human attribute of free will sustains self-worth. This concept is a binding one in the relationship between a Supreme Being and humanity that cannot be broken. One is totally free in exercising that will in decision making about anything. Do you recognize the power that free will gives to humans? The power of free will contributes significantly to the idea of the worth of every individual. Free will means decisions to break religious rules through behavior that offends God or others. When this occurs there must be a way to repair the damage and restore the sense of self-worth. God or Allah forgives forever. This certainly is an attribute of self-worth.

Another attribute of self-worth is the existence of the individual's soul. One may want to consider that the mind and the soul, our spiritual makeup that sustains life, are the same thing.

Therefore the mind, which is a spirit, is what lives on in eternity. If the soul lives in eternity it has no end. Therefore it is reasonable to infer that the individual soul has no beginning either but was in the mind of God and assigned to an individual at conception. This also is an attribute of self-worth.

The mind has a perfect potential in human existence although humanity, because of its limitations, inhibits the full expression of the mind during life. You may have noticed that there are some people who have an unusual sensitivity to others, even to the point of predicting future events that will occur, both good and bad. This is the operation of the perfect potential of the mind that is expressed sometimes by people whose human limitations are relaxed and do not interfere with the mind's expressions. This also is a characteristic of self-worth.

This brings up the subject of guilt, an inhibition with which many people are constantly bombarded. Shame is an associated feeling that can seriously interfere with social functioning and self-worth. Guilt is a normal function of the mind. It has the purpose of helping people who have committed some wrongdoing to be reminded not to do that same thing again. That is normative guilt.

Another form of guilt that is non-normative arises from concern about what others would feel or think if they knew what one's transgressions were. This guilt feels the same as normative guilt except than when analyzed there is no reality to the behavior that produced it. The foundation for the development of non-normative guilt usually is associated with developmental events such as being socialized into a rigid rule oriented form of behavior by parents or significant caretakers who were themselves very rigidly controlled.

An angry punitive parent or parents can generate a pervasive internal sense of guilt that will affect a sense of self-worth. Indifference, neglect and/or rejection experienced by children may result in a child feeling defective or that something is wrong with them. Internalization of a negative self may occur. These three occurrences in the developmental life of a child may be very harmful to feelings of self-worth. These feelings can be corrected through realistic thinking.

What has been described in this chapter is a description of self-worth and ways in which it may be sustained and increased. Hopefully clear thinking about events in one's life that leads to a positive perspective will be the result.

Chapter 10
Guilt and Shame

Guilt is an emotion or feeling, whether accurate or not, of having violated one's standard of behavior or a moral standard such as the Commandments. A standard of acceptable behavior is often established by association with others in which hurtful behavior toward any one of them produces guilt. Moral standards are rules for right and wrong behavior. They usually are established by religious belief and practice. Guilt may be moral or psychological although there is an overlap between the two. Moral guilt is often associated with religious belief about salvation and fear of punishment by God for sinful behavior. This belief may be associated with membership in a religious denomination in which fear of God is a dominant force. This may be a strong controlling factor in a person's life to the extent that it affects mental health. That is psychological guilt.

Guilt is a common theme in mental health as it usually is expressive of a state of conflict about what was done that shouldn't have been done or what was not done that should have been done. Remorse is an associated feeling that occurs following a behavior thought to be wrong. Remorse may lead to self-resentment and may be expressed through an apology, an attempt to repair damage and sometimes self-punishment.

There are types of guilt. The most obvious is a feeling of guilt for something one actually did that was wrong either because it was against a personal moral or ethical standard or because one caused physical or psychological harm to another person. Another is guilt for something you wanted to do even though you didn't. This is guilt provoking. A third is a feeling of guilt for something you think you did. Memories for past events are flawed so one may believe something wrong was done when it really wasn't. Feeling guilty over not having done enough to help someone is another type. For example, if you have a relationship with someone you've been helping for a long time and change in circumstances make it impossible to continue helping you may feel guilty. This feeling sometimes occurs among helping professionals. Feeling about being more successful than someone else also is a type of guilt.

Feelings of guilt are associated with socialization about accepted behavior. When this process of learning is rigid and punitive a child may internalize a rigid sense of self-control so even a slight deviation from an internalized rule can generate guilt. This may result in the formation of a negative self that will affect social functioning and interpersonal relationships.

A negative self may become internalized so that nothing seems worthwhile. These people may become socially isolated. They may follow an ordinary schedule of getting up in the morning and going to school or work but they don't become fully engaged in any activity. They may feel and act out of place. Their behavior is observed by others who may want to help but not knowing what to do ignore the problem and the person. This often has a further negative effect on persons who already feel uncomfortable in social situations so they withdraw even further.

Adherence to some religious beliefs and practices may have similar results. Group associations in which expectations of appropriate behavior are rigid and unbending may promote feelings of guilt when a thought of deviation from a rule occurs.

Feelings of guilt also may be produced by acts of indifference, neglect and rejection by primary or secondary attachment figures. Attachment to a primary attachment figure is an inherent need in all children. When this need is not met a child or adolescent may adopt an insecure attachment style that may be a longing for attachment that is expressed in dysfunctional behaviors. These behaviors mat interfere with interpersonal relationships.

Friends or associates also may produce feelings of guilt through negative comments or behavior. Ethnic and racial differences, difference in age, appearance and deviations from a perceived norm are other factors that may lead to feelings of guilt.

Emotional, physical and sexual abuse may cause feelings of guilt. Feelings that many children and adults have after negative emotional exchanges with significant others often are those of inferiority and inadequacy. These may be responsible for feelings of guilt because of self-blame over not being as good as others or not being as successful. Sexual abuse is demeaning. Physical abuse may have the same emotional effect. Both often result in confusion about the social position of the abuser that may generate guilt feelings.

Shame is a powerful emotion that can cause people to feel defective or unacceptable.

Shame may follow indifference, neglect or rejection by parents, friends or significant others. Self-esteem is learned through interaction with these people. The lack of self-esteem may generate feelings of shame.

Shame is an internal sense of being a bad person. Because this is emotionally painful a shamed person may try to keep it from being observed. For example, anger manages the fear of being seen as shameful. Portraying shame as embarrassment is another way to hide it.

Embarrassment is a less severe form of shame. The difference between shame and embarrassment is that shame does not necessarily involve public humiliation but embarrassment does. Shame is experienced as an internal feeling while embarrassment occurs with observation of others. Another coping mechanism is making fun of self in humor. Meeting the needs of others even when one's needs are not met hides shame as does trying to be perfect in what you do or maintaining an air of superiority.

Learning to manage guilt is a way to find relief from the emotional distress it causes.

Thinking realistically about why one has feelings of guilt is one approach. If you were raised in an environment where rigid and strict rules were applied in a punitive manner you may want to realize how neglected and rejected you felt. An internalized negative sense of yourself may have developed because you blamed yourself when your parents really were unrealistic. This may have resulted in a scrupulous conscience that is overbearing with guilt over many things for which guilt feelings are not realistic.

Relief from guilt consists of realizing the unreality of the behavior to which conformity was expected. Guilt is an emotion or feeling that may change with realistic thinking. Retraining feelings and changing behavior through thinking is possible.

Forgiving the self is a good idea. Life is such that behavior sometimes results from errors in judgment. Erroneous behavior associated with strong feelings that impede correct thinking and impulsive responses such as spontaneous anger following frustration do occur. Humans are basically good. Part of humanity is a struggle to do the right thing. Let up on yourself. You ;probably are doing better than you believe you are.

Managing shame is difficult. It requires a restoration of self-esteem. Being rejected creates a feeling of separation from others, a sense of shame and a loss of self-esteem. These feelings lead to dysfunctional behaviors that others don't understand so they avoid the shamed person. This reinforces the shamed individual's already self-negating feeling. Rethinking and relearning how perceptions of a negative self arose from being shamed is necessary. This may be accomplished through recalling shaming experiences that occurred during childhood and adolescence and recognizing that behavior was by others who may have been expressing their own feelings without recognizing the effect on the listener. This recall will require concentration. The persons who shamed the client likely were family members or close friends or religious authorities or teachers.

Remembering shameful incidents will require remembering perpetrators. These memories may create angry or hateful feelings that also could generate shame. These are just feelings that are never good or bad or right or wrong so there is no reason to feel shame.

Indifference, neglect and rejection often results in feelings of abandonment. When this is internalized, and it often is, the result may be a longing for the abandoning parent as a way to relieve feelings of guilt or shame. This longing is characterized by efforts to be in touch with a parent(s), to do things that serve them and attract positive attention and positive feedback from them. This will not solve the problem.

Remembering that your parents had issues that resulted in shaming behavior may be helpful. The release of feelings of vulnerability, fear and humiliation is the goal of remembering.

Thinking about the incidents in which shaming occurred may produce a different perspective.

If one recalls the details of these incidents it may become apparent that shaming is the behavior of another. The question then becomes what started the shaming. Who is responsible for the shaming behavior? What was said or done that was shaming? Is what was said or done realistic or the distorted, angry projection of the shaming person? Answers to these questions may shed light on the bad behavior of the other. When that is realized how realistic is your feeling of shame?

Understanding how shame affects a person helps release it. Overcoming the belief that one is bad takes time and exploration but it can be done. Some individuals can accomplish this by themselves but consulting a mental health professional who understands the process of shame release may be necessary. When shame release works and one learns assertiveness in expressing a positive self, self-esteem improves.

Self-esteem is often measured by comparison to others. A problem is that determining one's self-esteem through comparison to others fails to bolster one's self-esteem.

There always will be somebody perceived to have a more important social position or more or better worldly goods. It is every individual's uniqueness that gives worth and esteem. Therefore it is important to examine one's strengths and potential for accomplishment as indications of esteem.

Messages received from others affect self-esteem, especially when they are negative. An example is if you are chosen last for a team sport the view of others is that you are not very athletic. This is a shaming experience that diminishes self-esteem. He suggested that this results from the alacrity of accepting others' opinions. Managing shame is ceasing to live by the reflections of others and instead reflecting objectively on yourself and your strengths and weaknesses.

Humans are a combination of unique characteristics. What we learn as we develop determines self-esteem. Self-esteem is established when perceptions of these relationships are positive and internalized. If these relationships are characterized by indifference, neglect or rejection it is likely that what will be internalized is a negative sense of self. This may generate perceptions leading to assumptions or concepts about reality that are erroneous and decrease self-esteem. When a negative sense of self develops during developmental years a feeling of being a bad person may develop accompanied by loss of self-esteem. The blame for the indifferent, neglectful or rejecting attachment figure is assumed to be self-generated.

This negative sense is stored in the brain and continues to seek expression. It often is accompanied by negative thoughts about the self that affect self-esteem. These thoughts may generate more self-abasement and become a negative feedback loop that may lead to withdrawal from social contacts and suspiciousness about others. Restoring self-esteem is important in helping clients manage guilt and shame.

One way to manage shame is a restorative process, meaning working to restore the state of mind that existed before shaming incidents occurred. To clear the way for realistic thinking the first step in the process is to self-examine how you are coping with shame, either by blaming yourself, blaming others, withdrawing from social contacts or avoiding any discussion of how you feel. With this information you can consider whether these are working and what changes in yourself need to be made to find a workable answer. Reflecting on your feelings objectively may result in ceasing to blame the self through using ways to restore self-esteem that are suggested later in this chapter.

This objective thinking can help you to own your feeling of shame about which others know nothing unless you tell them or behave in a way that communicates your feeling. It also can help you to see that it is alright to avoid discussing your feelings openly because no one else needs to know how you feel except those who shamed you. Accepting your feeling can help to cease blaming others, especially if you consider that feelings are never good or bad or right or wrong. An objective analysis can restore self-esteem so you can see that no matter what shaming incidents occurred in your life does not diminish your worth.

Another part of the restorative process is a *restorative* conference that brings together those who have caused harm through shaming with those they have directly or indirectly harmed. Since shaming frequently occurs in families a restorative conference brings families together to discuss shaming experiences. This may be the most difficult part of the process because of anxiousness you might feel. However, if you have completed the first steps in the process you can approach the situation with confidence. The outcome will be either positive or negative. If it's positive that's good. If it's negative you can conclude those who shamed you have a negative attitude and that's on them. It's not your fault.

You can think realistically as an adult about assumptions and feelings made following any of the above experiences that may have occurred. Differentiating adult feeling from child feeling and developing a different perception of the experiences may then occur. This will promote a different and more realistic concept and likely free you from negative feeling, including guilt or shame. It is a way of improving and maintaining self-esteem.

Another way to increase self-esteem is for clients to stop comparing yourself to others. Think of your uniqueness, strengths and skills and give yourself credit for these attributes. Focus on the positives about yourself and your accomplishments. Forget and forgive yourself for the mistakes of the past.

Associate with others who share your beliefs and values. Help others whenever it is appropriate. Educate yourself professionally or technologically. If you are married and having problems get professional help.

Choose a vocation that fits your skills and be proud of your work and the contribution you make to the world. Remember that humanity needs a person to fill every work position and that your place in the scheme of things is an important square in the quilt of all the complex needs that must be met for the sake of advancing culture.

Religious beliefs and practices are another way to achieve and maintain self-esteem. Religiosity is significant in mental health and overall coping mechanisms that contribute to successful adaptation and social functioning. The link between religious belief and a positive self-esteem is real. It can be safely inferred that self-worth and self-esteem are integral parts of religious beliefs and practices.

It is safe to state that a feeling of self-esteem is related to a sense of being a good person. For clients that have religious beliefs and practices one way to measure this sense of goodness is following the Commandments that are accepted by many people in our culture. There is an aspect to the Commandments that can be quite comforting whether or not one believes in God. Many emotional and relationship problems arise from a lack of structure for behavior that the Commandments as rules can provide. The first three commandments refer to God but the last seven set limits on human behavior. They concern respect for parents, stealing, killing, false statements about others, adultery and taking another's goods or wife. All of these are serious transgressions that cover those behaviors that require rules that are part of structure. If one behaves following the

Commandments it is reasonable to believe that behavior will be normative and self-esteem will be maintained.

Another way of increase and sustain self-esteem is through prayer. There are formal prayers informal prayers that are infrequently verbalized but silently expressed. Research about prayer and its effect on the brain has suggested that prayer affects the brain in positive ways.

The human attribute of free will sustains self- esteem. One is totally free in exercising that will in decision making about anything. Do you recognize the power that free will gives to humans? The power of free will contributes significantly to self-esteem.

The subjects of guilt and shame presented here may be helpful to some people in deepening their understanding of the presence of guilt and shame in emotional distress and what might be done to relieve it.

Chapter 11
Anxiety, Defenses and Addictions

Anxiety is a prevailing condition in emotional distress. Anxiety and depression often occur together. Addiction is included in this chapter since substance abuse is prevalent in more than half of persons who have a mental health diagnosis. Often people become addicted to alcohol or drugs as a way of "medicating" both anxiety and depression. Substance abuse may provide short term relief for anxiety but becomes a more serious problem in the long term. Drinking alcoholic beverages tends to increase depression because alcohol is a depressive chemical.

Anxiety is a very uncomfortable feeling. It may be a concern about something bad happening, worry about health, or generalized worry about how well things are going.

There are many symptoms of anxiety, some mental and some physical. In many cases, symptoms include rushing thoughts, persistent ideas or phrases or songs or other compulsive thoughts. Physical symptoms include headaches, stomach aches, back aches, diarrhea and itching or pain that has no apparent physical cause. If any of these symptoms persist they should be checked by a physician who can determine if they are related to a real physical illness or an emotional problem.

Anxiety also may occur in obsessive ideas, compulsive behavior or phobias. Anxiety is pervasive and affects behavior and feelings almost every day. Many people say they cannot remember a time in their life when they didn't feel anxious. This is an indication that the feeling began very early in life.

Your mind is your friend and is at work for you to maintain a balance in your life. However, your mind can be affected by negative experiences so one may have to have corrective experiences in order to regain balance. Your mind protects you by reacting to any experience that produces anxiety through defense mechanisms.

Anna Freud, Sigmund Freud's daughter, wrote a book entitled *The Ego and the Mechanisms of Defense*. She described these mechanisms of defense as helping the ego, the conscious part of the personality, maintain a balance between the superego that contains ethical and moral behavior standards, the demands of the instincts of the id and reality. The ego, superego and id are the three parts of Freud's structure of the mind. Anxiety generally is a product of mental conflict between the parts of the mind. The mechanisms of defense act automatically to protect a person from the emotional pain of anxiety.

The mechanisms of defense that may occur include reversal, denial, regression, repression, reaction-formation, isolation, undoing, projection, introjection, displacement, turning against the self, and sublimation. Defense mechanisms do not by themselves solve the conflict but can help social functioning when they work. Any behavior or thought that is employed specifically to fend off anxiety can be considered a defense. One problem is that defenses take a great deal of energy to maintain. This requirement decreases the amount of energy available for other mental and physical functions.

It is important to understand that removing defenses may not be appropriate as the conflicts they are managing can become active without them. The appropriate action is to consult a mental health professional to resolve the conflict so the defenses are not necessary.

Both children and adults can develop a structured set of defenses. This means that the way they feel and think is fixed in their mind and used frequently as a way to control anxiety. Often this strategy is successful so changing it is not a good idea. A brief description of Anna Freud's defense mechanisms follows.

Regression is a temporary or long-term return of the ego to an earlier stage of development to avoid managing unacceptable impulses. Repression involves pushing uncomfortable thoughts or memories to an inaccessible area of the mind. They may reappear as an unknown anxiety or dysfunctional behavior and can also reappear through dreams or slips of the tongue. Reaction formation is a defense mechanism in which the perception of certain feelings or desires is socially or legally unacceptable. This is employed to convince others of the opposite, usually in an exaggerated way. Isolation is a defense that involves creating a space between an unpleasant or threatening cognition and other thoughts and feelings.

By minimizing associative connections with other thoughts the threatening cognition is remembered less often and is less likely to affect self-esteem or the self concept. Introjection is a defense in which a person internalizes the ideas or values of others. An example is internalizing a negative sense of self as a result of indifference, neglect or rejection by a primary attachment figure. Displacement is the transfer of a negative emotion from one person or thing to an unrelated person or thing. An example is anger at the boss that is taken home and acted out or transferred toward a spouse or another family member. Another form of displacement is "turning-against-self" when the anger is redirected toward the self instead of another object. This may be associated with depression and suicide. Reversal is a defense mechanism in which one changes behavior to its opposite. For example, masochism, the tendency to derive pleasure from pain is replaced by sadism, the tendency to derive pleasure from inflicting pain on another. Denial is a defense in which one refuses to accept the reality of a painful experience or uncomfortable thoughts and feelings as if they did not occur. It is said to be primitive because its development is rooted in early childhood. Sublimation as a defense occurs where there is a transfer of unwanted impulses into something that is less harmful. It channels the energy associated with managing uncomfortable thoughts away from destructive acts and into something that is more socially acceptable. An example is beating a rug as a way of relieving anger.

Anxiety is different from fear although it's sometimes hard to tell the difference. Anxiety is internal and results from emotional conflict. The source of anxiety may be difficult to discover. Many anxious people seek mental health services to uncover the source and deal with it is more effectively. Fear occurs with observation. For example, if you are about to cross a street and you observe an oncoming vehicle the fear of being struck and possibly killed or injured prevents you from stepping into traffic.

The word anxiety is generally a diagnostic term so the term "anxiousness" may be more appropriate in many cases. Anxiousness is largely a normal response to a worrisome experience. Only when a person is so anxious that it interferes with normative adaptation and social functioning is it a problem for which some mental health assistance should be sought. Many people normally get anxious when facing a new experience or one that has some perceived potential threat. Visits to a dentist or a physician conjure up such a reaction. Being called to the boss's office or receiving a message that's not good news can bring the same response.

The root of anxiety resides, for the most part, in the relationship between the child or adolescent and a primary attachment figure. Physical or emotional separation from this figure for whatever reason generates a feeling of anxiety because of the sense of loss. This separation may occur when the primary caretaker, almost always the mother, is indifferent neglectful or rejecting of a child. These losses generally are felt as abandonment, a feeling that is a threat to the conscious self and can become stored in the emotional center of the brain. This feeling will continuously seek expression and can result in self-blame and anxiety. Once developed, it generates a neural pathway that can remain constant until a corrective experience generates a new pathway.

Many anxiety producing experiences occur when we are very young and unable to do something to help ourselves. Sometimes the resulting anxiousness can be managed by self-soothing, a skill that develops over time. However, some people never seem to learn this skill very well. These people will generally be more anxious, worry more about things and have a more difficult time adapting to reality.

There are some instances when the level of anxiety is so strong that it produces excessive suspicions about others' negative attitudes and behaviors. Should this occur, consult a mental health professional and follow her/his recommendations.

With some effort and the assistance of reading this book you may recall the reasons for feeling anxious. An example is being born into a family situation where mother had to work to support the family and was not able to give you the attention that you needed. *Accept such facts as real and that <u>this wasn't your fault</u>.* Live in the moment and focus on whatever you are doing without letting distracting negative thoughts enter your mind. Recognize the source of the anxiousness and examine the facts of what is happening now. This reality orientation generally provides a sense of calm. See what you are doing? You are *thinking*. When you think about the reality of anxious feelings, control over them will increase. Remember, no one grows up perfectly normal so you have a lot of company in the people around you.

It may be helpful to consider the difference between normal and normative behavior. Normative behavior is that behavior that observers generally would approve. It is not necessarily normal behavior. What is normal for one social group may not be normal for another. For example, if one is a member of a criminal gang, criminal behavior is normative, although not normal to most observers.

The bell curve in statistics is another example. About 68% of the area under the curve falls within one standard deviation. About 95% of the area under the curve falls within two standard deviations. About 99.7% of the area under the curve falls within three standard deviations. This suggests 68% of people have a normal distribution of anxiety. Twenty seven percent (27%) have a mild increase because of ordinary events and five percent (5%) a more serious anxiety. This suggests the percent of abnormal behavior from average is rather small. What might this mean? How is it useful? Well for one thing those people who are anxious about themselves and what others think about them can stop worrying so much. Although you may have some anxious moments there is very little possibility others see anything abnormal or non-normative about your behavior. Nobody can read your mind. This is the beginning of thinking rather than feeling.

Anxiety may be a serious problem for school age children. It can cause them to be fidgety and distracted in school. More than one child exhibiting these behaviors has been incorrectly labeled as ADHD (attention-deficit/hyperactivity disorder) by a teacher who observes the distracting behavior. This can often result in a child being prescribed medication for ADHD when anxiousness is the real issue.

If the prescribed medication doesn't make a difference in behavior after the time required for the drug to take effect, further investigation of the reason for the problem should be considered. Anxiety, not ADHD is the likely cause. Anxiety causes much of what is considered dysfunctional behavior. Anxiety interferes with functioning so it's harder to think straight, to make good judgments, remember things, learn, make friends, think clearly, postpone gratification and see reality for what it is.

There sometimes are social situations that increase anxiety. For example, someone may say something negative to you, either critical or mean. When this happens you need to view carefully the whole situation. If a remark is considered to be negative, what is the context in which it occurred? If the remark was made by a person in authority, is there truth to it? If so, a correction in your thinking or behavior may need to be made. Some persons in authority lack the skill to make corrective statements. Consider the source and respond accordingly. If you are a sensitive person, remind yourself of your vulnerability and don't take it personally.

In every situation, try to analyze the context. Consider the elements of the situation and how they affect what is being expressed by the people in it. Practically every event in one's life occurs in some context. Other people may be involved so understanding the context in which an event has produced a negative feeling is important. Once you understand the context, it will be easier to analyze it. Watch the expression on people's faces. Listen accurately to what they say and be objective in your interpretation. When you get a good grasp of the context in your situation, you will be more quickly able to see why certain things are said. If you are tempted by spontaneous thought to take something personally *think* carefully about why that is. These cautions can make conversations more meaningful.

Sometimes people learn from a heavy-handed parent. This may occur when a child is socialized, meaning when they are taught the general rules of behavior and how to get along with others. If caretakers are rigid in rule making and frequently punitive and harsh to a child, that child will internalize more rigid rule-oriented behaviors which can be both a positive and a negative. The positive is that these individuals, because they are driven to some extent, try hard to do the right thing and often are successful. The negative side is that some develop an inner sense that can lead to seeing every questionable behavior as either wrong or sinful. This increases anxiousness. But, as you will learn, this too can be changed by clear *thinking*.

There is a saying: "put your brain in gear before you put your mouth in motion."

This saying can apply to most every situation. If you are the recipient of someone's unkind remark think about the fact that this may be produced by their inability to think before speaking. It also may come from anxiousness they have about something that has occurred in their life. It is important to realize that anytime a disappointing or traumatic event occurs, a lot of energy is spent managing or coping with it. The result can be that energy is not available to control other mental and physical functions and so a person may say or do something irrational that they wouldn't otherwise say or do.

Trauma in childhood is likely to have a long term effect on personality development. A child's inability to manage the fear of trauma has a disabling effect on social functioning. Trauma is an unusually frightening experience such as witnessing the death of someone close.

Anger often is a part of the reaction and is an emotion that often manages fear. This may lead to a "short temper" or quick, angry reactions to things. This often occurs in persons who have inferior feelings about themselves.

Sometimes frustration occurs with anxiousness about someone's aggressive statement or behavior. This occurs based on the frustration-aggression principle which suggests that an aggressive response occurs automatically to a frustrating event. The response is spontaneous and therefore not easy to control. However, if one tries to self-discipline, to think before they act, this can help.

Understand that anxiousness is very common. Some of it results from the culture because of a focus on competition. Competition is learned at a very young age and drives many people to succeed. However, it also is responsible for many becoming very anxious because they don't feel good enough or because they feel that they are just like the rest of the crowd. Competition occurs often at youth sports events where parents become overly excited about a play especially when their child is involved. In high school, theme songs at sporting events are often called fight songs and many cheers have the word "fight" in them which implies aggressive behavior that can lead to anxious feelings.

One may wonder how much different our culture would be if we focused on cooperation and working together to achieve desired ends. How much better off would people be if they were valued for what they can contribute even if the level of contribution is not equal to others? Perhaps you were overweight as a youth so you were chosen last to be on a team because of the perception that the team had to win and that you may not be suited to help the team meet that goal. Unfortunately, coaches or team leaders tend to choose those they perceive are the best for the task. No one seems to care if feelings are hurt or that being chosen last can result in adopting inadequate feelings of self.

One may ask why teams cannot simply play against each other just for the fun of it. In high school and college and even in some elementary schools, being the best team in the league is highly sought. Certain players are chosen for honors while others who made significant contributions may receive no recognition at all. Remember, recognition lasts a very short time while damage done to a person's self-esteem can be long lasting.

Addiction to various behaviors or substances is a problem for many people. The actions being taken to manage addictions are not solving the problem but instead are making it worse. It has been observed that about two-thirds of those persons that have had emotional or mental adjustment reactions are substances abusers.

Addiction can be a condition resulting from ingesting a substance, i.e. alcohol, drugs, or engaging in an activity (e.g., gambling, sex) that is pleasurable but the continued use of which becomes compulsive and therefore interferes with ordinary life responsibilities. It often is difficult to determine how the addiction began. It could have been accidental or on purpose, suggested by friend or for other reasons. With some addictions the pleasure associated with the behavior leads to accelerated use until the point where one is dependent upon whatever the substance or behavior is. People have the ability to think about the outcomes of behavior but do not do so for any number of reasons.

What do people with an addiction look like? What is their lifestyle? Many would quickly answer with a stereotypical picture. They are "down and out," "misfits," "social outcasts." Common sense suggests that isn't the case. There are addicts who function well enough so as not to be identified as such while there are others who do not function well at all. There also are those that function marginally but are protected by those around them. Their real problem never is apparent. Addiction includes a rather broad spectrum of persons.

There are at least two points of view about the nature of addiction. One is that it is a disease that requires medical treatment. The other is that it is an emotional disorder that is being "medicated" by the addictive substance. There is disagreement about this as it is too simplistic but the point is that addictive behavior is likely an adaptation or a defense that manages negative feelings about self. It doesn't work and in fact usually results in added depression because of the effect of the chemicals (drugs, alcohol etc.) or behaviors that may be involved.

This suggests that there is a common thread involved in addictive behavior which is a feeling of being disconnected from the surrounding world. The ingestion of addictive materials or other addictive behaviors is an adaptation to a feeling of being alone in the world or a reaction to an environment where indifference, neglect and/or rejection have been significant experiences.

Other parts of this book have discussed individual reactions to indifference, neglect and rejection. This environment creates neural pathways in the brain that are stored in the emotional center. These feelings seek to be expressed. When they are expressed the behavior that follows a is based on anxiousness. The individual may become overly suspicious about the reactions of others. Anxiousness about the self can bring a person to the point of believing others are responding in a negative way which can be very uncomfortable. Some find relief through behaviors that may become addictive if used habitually. These may include consuming alcohol, using illicit drugs, prescription drug abuse, smoking, gambling or illicit sex.

One may question whether treatment programs have been properly designed to help addicts. Many are inpatient for 28 days. The recidivism or return rate suggests something may be missing. Substance abuse or addiction is viewed as a disease so persons being treated are considered "sick." If one is sick that is non-normative. If one is non-normative that is different and quite likely to produce an indifferent, neglectful and/or rejecting response by others. The person is discharged and returns to the previous environment. What's changed? The addict is right back in the same place as before treatment facing the same individuals and situations.

There is a larger picture at work here. What is characteristic of our culture is that it fails to provide a supportive environment. Supportive environment is discussed more fully in another chapter. Our culture promotes competition rather than cooperation. Success is often measured by the amount of material goods one has. Driving the best car, living in the nicest neighborhood and wearing the most fashionable clothes are included in these measurements. Striving to succeed does not promote a supportive environment. Instead it promotes people distancing themselves from each other. Family living close to each other, that may create a supportive environment, has decreased. People that are different from each other such as age, sex, ethnicity and race difference, often do not find a supportive environment. People who have been in jail or prison and people who have a mental illness often don't either. These multiple situations exist in a competitive culture that also often doesn't provide a supportive environment.

These conditions of life can set the stage for persons who are vulnerable and who create an adaptive strategy that includes a set of mental defenses developed in order to survive. Among the adaptive strategies is the tendency to abuse substances; to drink too many alcoholic beverages; to use an illegal drug or misuse prescription medication. The temporary relief from the emotional pain associated with being in a non-supportive environment can become habitual and eventually addictive.

The phenomenon of a supportive environment was studied using laboratory rats. One study involved a single rat in a cage with two bottles, one containing a drug and the other one containing water. The rat chose the drug and drank continuously from that bottle until it died from an overdose. A second study involved group of rats placed in a cage in which everything was provided for them. There also was two bottles, one with a drug and the other with water. All the rats tried both bottles. The group divided itself into those that shunned the drug and those that didn't. The group of rats favoring the drug included those who didn't take advantage of all the toys and activities in the cage and became heavy users of the drug. A third experiment involved rats that were heavy drug users. They were taken out of isolation, placed in the cage where food, toys and activities were provided. They eventually stopped taking the drug and lived normally. The results of these experiments suggest that a supportive environment made the difference in whether or not the rats chose the drug. The same choices are made by humans.

Soldiers returning from Vietnam demonstrated the effect of choice. Although many became addicted to heroin most stopped taking the drug when they returned home where they had a supportive environment. Physicians have experienced the same situation in patients for whom they prescribed heroin. When there no longer was a need for the drug, these patients just stopped taking it. A reasonable explanation for this outcome in the case of the soldiers is that addiction to the drug was a way of adapting to the non-supportive environment of war. Returning home to a supportive environment made that adaptive strategy unnecessary. In the case of the medical patients, the use of a drug did not mean the loss of a supportive environment but rather it was part of a treatment program.

The evidence from these experiments suggested that a supportive environment in which a connection with others is significant should be included in the planning of a strategy to combat substance abuse. There are many facets to this problem, so a comprehensive plan is needed.

Often people do not admit abusing substances. Treatment of substance abuse can be very challenging. Often persons who have this disorder are medicating themselves for anxiety. While anxiety may have originally led to the addictive behavior, addiction is now the real problem. It is important to get as many support mechanisms in place as possible. The family or significant other, should be involved. Attending AA regularly is highly recommended. After treatment, it is desirable to manage the anxiety to prevent a potential addictive relapse.

Some things for a reader to consider when seeking treatment for a substance abuse disorder are: a mental health provider should provide help even if one is under the influence during a session; a provider should encourage a client to develop a secure attachment to the clinician by being available for telephone calls, emergency sessions, reaching out when necessary and appropriate, keeping appointments, and being honest and forthright. Relationship is a major factor with the client learning to trust if recovery is to be the outcome.

Chapter 12
Feeling and Thinking

Any valid discussion of mental health issues has to make reference to feelings as they often contribute significantly to behavior. Human nature is such that people are sensitive to feelings. Children are especially vulnerable to the behaviors and reactions of others toward them. Interaction with others makes a significant impression on a child's mind. As is discussed elsewhere in this book negative experiences create neural pathways in the brain that will influence decisions about behavior throughout life unless new positive experiences of a similar nature generate new neural pathways as replacements. This is why changes in adaptation and social functioning are so important.

People are different in the amount of acceptance and nurturing they need to feel comfortable. Likewise, parents are different in their capacity to provide care and nurturing for children. This mix of characteristics can sometimes be responsible for feeling self-conscious or negative about the self. Whatever "feeling" problems might arise because of negative experiences, they are not the fault of either the parent or the child. However, often one or the other feels guilty and this can add to the problem. If you see yourself in this description think about not being at fault. Sometimes a conversation with a parent if you are the child or with the child if you are a parent may help clarify feelings.

Feelings are not easy to define. One definition is that feelings are a state of mind. Perhaps the more important question is: how do feelings begin? How are they formed? Often feelings and emotions are viewed as equals, but are they? Some refer to feeling as thinking. Since the definition is somewhat difficult to make with certainty, a definition of feeling for the purpose of this book is appropriate. Feeling is a spontaneous affective (emotional) response of the mind to external or internal stimuli. Thinking is a deliberate exercise of the mind directed toward the analysis of external or internal stimuli.

Based upon these definitions, it is easy to see that one cannot feel and think at the same time.

Demonstrations of this proposition are not difficult to find. For example, a frustrating experience generally results in an immediate angry response. However, if you can interrupt this response by *thinking* about the frustrating event the response can be controlled. This is not easy but it is possible.

Feelings are spontaneous and can be quite strong. Sometimes they are rational and sometimes not. Rational feelings have a reality base and generally there is a follow through with them. Those feelings that are irrational generally are not related to some current event or perception but arise from some past internalized emotional experience. For example, a rational emotional response is one that occurs following a positive interpretation of a behavior. Someone you respect tells you that you are doing well with a particular behavior, such as the boss complimenting your work on a project. You feel the respect and are gratified emotionally for it.

The same is true for someone who tells you something negative about yourself. You feel criticized and you may be angry about it. Then you examine the feeling and make a decision about it. This examination is *thinking*. Feelings can generate all sorts of positive or negative responses. However, what you *think* about them is what is the most responsible for an appropriate behavioral response.

We learn from experience. Often experiences can lead to erroneous assumptions. When this happens, self-defeating and negative self-thoughts may occur. How we interpret experiences is what can be disturbing. People and things do not distress us. It's what we believe about them that generates problem feelings. Realizing this and *thinking* about it can make a big difference.

One problem with feelings is they often call for a judgment. This can be tricky since judgments about the self is difficult enough. Judging others is unrealistic. It's like saying you understand somebody who's different from you. However, if you cannot demonstrate what you say you understand, you really don't understand. This is a mistake many make when not *thinking*.

Judgments often are made about ourselves and others because of the mix of feelings that occur around various events in life. People who are the victims of the judgments often feel criticized or rejected which can be hurtful to them.

What did you feel when a criticism or rejection occurred to you? Did you have negative feelings? Did you have self-doubts? Did you wonder how others felt about you? Did you try hard to behave in a way that earned approval from others or did you have a behavior problem, acting out in frustration, losing your temper or staying angry? Did you feel depressed, rejected, lonely and sad?

If you had some of these feelings, who did you blame for them? If you are a mature adult you may have thought about whether the criticism or rejection was justified. If you believed it was justified you then may have thought about what change in behavior might be made to avoid such an experience in the future. You may have just ignored it. You may have asked the person why they were critical or rejecting so you could understand. You may have blamed the person or shrugged it off, thinking that they are just being negative.

You may have had one of the reactions described above. It is highly likely that what you did was related to how you were treated by those responsible for you as you were growing up. You may have had mixed feelings about what to do kin response to their indifferent, rejecting or neglectful behavior. Blaming them at the time may have made your relationship with them worse immediately. Given these situations there were two possible choices: blame them or blame the self. Children are smart enough to know that blaming parents does not help so they blame themselves. That can lead to an inferiority complex. Sometimes a child or adolescent will develop a particular problem behavior or conduct disorder related to difficult parent relationships.

Behavior and conduct disorders can be difficult to manage. Often there is a sense of defiance in the child. Lack of respect for parents and for behavioral rules may occur. Most of the time children who act out behaviorally are expressing an increased level of anxiousness. This may be triggered in a child when the child is feeling threatened or fearful. Anger manages fear. Fear of rejection, physical or emotional punishment or the loss of someone or something significant may be factors.

Sometimes this reaction may be fear of losing a parent through death or divorce, illness of a parent, possible hospitalization of a significant family member, heated arguments between parents, bullying by other children, disagreements between or among children in the family, etc.

Sometimes children's behavioral problems extend to the school. Often teachers are frustrated and seek ways to maintain control by suggesting that a child be evaluated for attention deficit hyperactivity disorder (ADHD). While this may be true, the differential diagnosis between ADHD and anxiety is often difficult to make. Medication for ADHD is often prescribed when the real reasons for acting out behavior are due to anxiety. Careful evaluation by a professional who assesses and treats ADHD is essential. Sometimes a second opinion is important so the right diagnosis and treatment are provided.

It is essential to recognize that whatever feelings you have, even those that are the most negative, resentful or harmful, cannot be judged. Common sense suggests, if you *think* about it, that whatever is learned from experience is a result of that experience. That doesn't mean you don't have a responsibility to correct those feelings if they affect your social functioning.

Feelings of guilt deserve some attention. If indifference, neglect or rejection has occurred in your life, you may feel guilty even though you don't understand why. Children want to please their parents, but if parents are unresponsive children wonder why. They tend to look internally, feeling it's their fault. Guilt can be the natural result. These feelings can linger on into adulthood.

Loss often is a difficult feeling. Perhaps, it's a feeling that something is missing in your life. Maybe it's a vague sense of lack of fulfillment. Maybe it's an empty feeling, a feeling you should have done something but didn't, or you lost something and can't remember what it was. These feelings often arise from a loss of a close relationship with a parent. They can be felt as a loss of self-esteem or a loss of self-confidence, but either way these are difficult feelings that tend to be on your mind more than you desire.

Death of a person to whom you feel attached brings a strange feeling. You feel disconnected. You don't feel like you fit. You may feel left out or abandoned. Separation anxiety can generate feelings of loneliness and sadness. This comes from a lack of attachment, from which anxiousness can develop. This is painful and often leads to irrational decisions about how it can be managed. This can lead to abusing alcohol or other substances. Self-medication is a way of reducing the pain. Usually this is successful only in the short run and may lead to habits of behavior that are dysfunctional and self-destructive. .Seeing a grief counselor may be helpful.

If you are inclined to substance abuse it is important to figure out why. Alcohol and drugs can lead to the suppression of difficult feelings. However, substance abuse contributes to underlying depressive feelings so in the long run this is not a successful way to feel better.

A major problem with substance abuse is that these substances can be addictive. This leads to physical desires for them that may result in serious physical illness and sometimes death. If friends or family tell you have alcohol or drug problem, they may be suggesting that these substances are affecting your social functioning. It's a good idea to listen and to get help with the problem. There are many good sources for treatment of substance addiction.

Going out of one's way to be helpful to others is generally observed to be a good characteristic. However, this can be an effort to control anxiety and may also be a way of convincing the self that others appreciate the effort to help and hence may like and respect you more for your actions. Many people who behave this way have a history of indifference, neglect or rejection, sometimes sexual abuse from attachment figures. However, it may provide others with an opportunity to take advantage of your good will. When this happens there may be a lot of effort and money going to support a cause that is never ending. The benefactor of this good will is typically a very dependent person with serious personal deficits who has learned the advantages associated with dependency and does everything they can to ensure the dependency continues. This means the giver may get stuck in a relationship that will be disappointing much of the time yet very difficult to discontinue. Sometimes dependency will provoke hostility which generates a whole new set of problems.

Abandonment and engulfment are two major feeling problems for children. Abandonment can leave a person with a feeling of not being good enough which can extend itself into practically every area of human relationships. It may be internalized with an accompanying sense of hopelessness which is real and persistent. The core element in these experiences is the loss of attachment to caretakers. Death of a parent may be another contributing factor in feeling abandoned. Sometimes one or both parents are incapacitated through substance abuse. Sometimes children are born to teens that aren't ready to have a child. Feelings of abandonment often occur to children in these circumstances. Dealing with this feeling can be successful if one *thinks* that difficult things occur in life that should not be taken personally. If the feeling persists talking with a mental health professional may help.

Engulfment is not a word that is used frequently in ordinary conversation. In this case, engulfment refers to over attention given to a child by a caregiver or attachment figure. Engulfment may be more stressful than abandonment as the overly attentive reactions by a caretaker may be a way of managing their anger and rejection toward a child. Engulfment may include caution beyond reason and restrictions that keep a child from learning and growing emotionally. Engulfment may be a way of managing guilt about not liking a child but denying this negative feeling through overextending attention and care. Children don't understand this but they do react to it. The reality is that most children pick up the caretaker's negative underlying attitude toward them. They get confused because this feeling is not out in the open so there is no available way to fight it. This kind of indirect rejection generally has a more devastating effect on a child than direct rejection. If you recognize these feelings in yourself this explanation may help bring them out in the open. If that is too difficult talking to a mental health professional may be necessary.

A child's persistent angry feeling is another issue. The source of the anger should be considered. If a child does not receive the amount of attention needed, one of the consequences may be anger. The anger sometimes becomes so strong that aggressive thoughts occur especially toward the person who has abused or abandoned a child. These temper tantrums are the rage of the inner child and can be frightening. Sometimes a child cannot express angry feelings because of the fear of being rejected. This can generate a lot of emotional pain. When any type of abuse has occurred to a child, anger and resentment may develop. This anger or resentment may be directed toward the primary caretaker or attachment figure since the child expected that the primary attachment figure should have protected her/him from the abuse. This anger may persist because of confusion. A child knows intuitively that expressing anger likely will create more problems so the child says nothing. This allows the anger to fester into adulthood. It is very important that children who have been abused are given psychological help to learn how to manage their confused feelings in a way that doesn't interfere with normative social functioning.

The presence of suicidal ideas should be questioned.

Have you ever been rejected? Have you failed a test in school? Did you finish last in a competitive event? Recall that your feelings probably weren't very positive. How did you react? Did you feel bad? How did you get over these bothersome feelings?

Rejection is generally unpleasant but it happens to just about everybody at some time. It's important when one experiences rejection to think about the circumstances in context. If you are a sensitive person you probably experienced indifference, neglect or rejection in your early life. If so you may have been conditioned to react more strongly and perhaps overreact to any form of rejection. Think about that first. If you do have a tendency to overreact then separate that reaction from the current experience by controlling your feeling through *thinking* about the reality of what has happened. Perhaps you are being overly sensitive when what you perceived as a rejection was really a comment by somebody who has your best interest at heart. Perhaps it was a comment by a person in authority who has a responsibility to supervise your work. Perhaps the rejection came from somebody who rejects everybody or is just a mean thoughtless person. There are many reasons like this for a rejecting event to occur. *Think*. Is it realistic? Who is responsible? Why would that person say or do what they did? *Thinking* will change things. *Thinking* about feelings will be easier if the organized process of *context, explanation and thinking* described in Chapter 5 is applied. Some of the content of that process is repeated in the next paragraphs.

Context is a way of reviewing the effects of developmental and environmental experiences on adaptation and social functioning. Remember that adaptation is successful management of internal desires, impulses and instincts as well as external interpersonal relationships. Social functioning is behavior in a social situation that observers would accept as normative. Context provides a clearer picture of a person's strengths and weaknesses. Knowledge of these factors can result in a more objective perspective in which context can be viewed as contributing to a problem. It also helps to differentiate between child and adult feelings. Child feelings are those stored in the emotional center of the brain that seek expression. Adult feelings are those in the present. Achieving this understanding by itself can bring considerable relief and also provide an opportunity for feelings about the situation to become secondary to *thinking* about how one can progress toward normative social functioning. Knowledge of context enables one to assess how emotional problems arise through developmental events and the social environment in which the problem developed. This can provide a transition to explanation.

Explanation is a reflection on *Context*, especially the nature of a person's attachment to the primary and secondary attachment figures. The purpose of this reflection is to promote *thinking* about the impact of the factors explored in *context* or how developmental and environmental factors are the background for emotional problems. *Thinking*, the third phase of the process, can help to explain how what happened during the *context* phase has affected adaptation and social functioning. Reflection may be easier if one understands the Attachment Behavioral System that was described previously. It is activated when there is a threat of separation from the attachment figure, whether physical or emotional. If the attachment figure is not nearby or is unresponsive the attached person will display anxious behaviors that continue until the attachment figure returns and pays attention to the child or adult. You probably have experienced this in your own life and recall the anxious feelings about separation or loss. If a separation from the attachment figure occurred during the early developmental years it may affect a person's adaptation and social functioning throughout life unless changed through mental health intervention.

Internal working models, or mental representations, are expectations and beliefs about the self and others. They were established in the first few years of life and become increasingly resistant to change. If a child is feeling bad and gets a caring response from a loving adult, a feeling of deserving of being loved happens along with the sense that others will help and protect when problems arise. A negative or uncaring response from an attachment figure will produce an internal working model of that figure as rejecting which can lead to a feeling of being unworthy with others not expected to provide help and support. Bowlby also proposed that those persons who feel good about themselves expect others to respond positively to them. Those who expect rejection and have low self esteem tend to distance themselves from others.

Thinking follows *Explanation*. The objective is to change the original feeling reactions to adverse developmental and environmental events that led to assumptions of self-depreciation and internalized negative feelings about self. Explanation provides a framework for thinking about reactions to developmental and environmental experiences. A new perspective can develop through thinking about these experiences along with an awareness of the prospect of change in assumptions and feelings that will lead to change in behavior.

In summary the model begins with context or the gathering of all relevant factors that have contributed to emotional distress. This is followed by explanation for which the objective is to provide a practical and reasoned approach to explain the pathway that led to the development of emotional difficulties. During thinking one will rethink and relearn using knowledge gleaned during the explanation phase. The objective is to provide a reality orientation to these events so there is relief from negative and dysfunctional feelings and behaviors.

Readers also should be aware of mindfulness. It is a state of mind in which one focuses on being aware of and accepting feelings, thoughts and physical sensations in the present. It sometimes is used as part of treatment for emotional distress. It also means that there is no judgment about feelings or thoughts. There only is a focus on the present.

There are several benefits to mindfulness. Some examples are: it is good for the body as it improves the immune system and reduces stress; good for the mind as it increases positive emotions; good for the brain as it increases regulation of emotions, empathy, learning and memory. It increases altruism and understanding of the problems of others.

These are some suggestions about practicing mindfulness. Pay close attention to your breathing. Focus on the sights, smells and sound senses you're experiencing at the moment. Know that your thoughts and feelings, no matter what they are, are short lived and do not define you as a person; focus on body sensations such as the way you sit in a chair. There are mindfulness centers in many urban areas where professionals engage in training of mindfulness.

This chapter dealt with feelings and *thinking*. From reading it you may have learned something about both. You may also have learned that the others' expressions of feelings come from them. You may also have developed a way of *thinking* by knowing that feelings are just feelings and are not right or wrong, good or bad and cannot be judged. Perhaps, you also have learned something about *thinking* and how it can help develop a new perspective about feelings.

Thinking or cognition really is different from emotion or feeling. *Thinking* requires rationality. It also requires facts. If a person didn't have a positive start in life and internalized a negative sense of self all sorts of inadequate feelings will come to mind constantly. Many of these feelings will be characteristic of a lack of self-esteem. Question whether these feelings are rational or factual. *Think*. Perhaps they are erroneous interpretations of events.

We don't often reflect on the power of the mind and the enormous capacity and flexibility of the human brain. Similarly we frequently don't consider learning as a major part of life. Every experience a person has results in learning even though the exact process of how humans learn is not well understood. There are several learning theories, but they are descriptive mostly of the process of teaching and conditions under which people appear to learn. The best thing a person can learn is how to *think*. Among other attributes this means an ability to comprehend the real meaning of any proposition or statement whether verbal or in writing. One educational theorist believes that the highest levels of learning are analysis, synthesis and evaluation. Analysis is the ability to break down an expression into its parts. Synthesis puts these parts together in a new way that expresses a meaning which fits the statement or problem at hand. Evaluation is the application of what is synthesized to the resolution of a problem situation as a test of whether the *thinking* process produced accurate results. The results may not always be what one wants but that isn't the point. It is true meaning that is sought.

Feelings are very often the basis for behavior. Every person has a wide scope of feelings.

The mind has a tremendous capacity for storing feelings which can be positive or negative. A person develops a feeling around experience. Negative feelings continue to seek consciousness and may be very troublesome. They contribute to an internal negative sense of self that often appears in negative self-feelings such as "I'm not good enough"; "I can't do that"; "I'm not very good looking"; and other similar feelings. These negative feelings interfere with adaptation and social functioning.

Sometimes the feelings are repressed, especially if the event is traumatic. Repression is an unconscious mental defense mechanism that works automatically to keep feelings out of consciousness that would generate anxiety. There is a similar mental process entitled suppression that is a conscious effort to put feelings aside in the active mind so they have little or no effect on behavior. This isn't always successful. Repressed feelings may appear suddenly when a trigger experience similar to the original trauma occurs as these feelings continuously seek expression. Some of them form the basis of inappropriate behavior.

The mind cannot *think* and feel at the same time. It is structured in a way that prevents simultaneous cognitive and emotive activity. *Thinking* is a rational and deliberate process while feelings are spontaneous and sometimes irrational. You can test this for yourself. If you feel angry about something think about why you are angry or about the consequences of expressing the anger irrationally. If you are successful in thinking, the angry feeling will dissipate. The same thing is true of other feelings. A principle of cognitive theory suggests that if you feel depressed, think of something pleasant or rewarding and the depression should lift. *Think* differently about a distressing issue to diminish negative emotion. This is not so easy to do but it does work.

Two factors in life that affect us every day are adaptation and social functioning. Adaptation is often thought of as a coping mechanism. Adaptation was defined as the ability to manage internal drives and instincts as well as successfully managing interpersonal relationships and environmental challenges. Humans are bombarded regularly by a variety of feelings. Some are realistic and some not. Often the inner child is seeking expression so feelings are immature and interfere with positive adaptation. How one manages adaptation and the building of skills that lead to success can affect their level of social functioning.

Thinking rather than feeling can produce an entirely different outcome. Feelings are just feelings. They are never good or bad, right or wrong. Some can argue saying they "feel bad" which is quite different. One may feel "bad" but the feeling itself is not bad.

Memories of experiences with parents early in life often leave an indelible mark on the brain and these memories may be transferred to other individuals. You probably can recall meeting a person to whom you are immediately attracted and with whom you feel comfortable. Conversely you may meet someone you immediately don't like. You cannot explain why these reactions occur. However, the reason may be a connection between something about the other person who exhibits a trait similar to that of one or both of your parents or attachment figures. Knowing that such a reaction could occur makes it possible to think clearly about your responses to other persons.

It is essential if one is to maintain effective social functioning to avoid behaving spontaneously to feelings. Putting one's mind in gear before putting one's mouth in motion is taken from a well known saying. The same applies to behavior. This means *thinking* about a feeling before acting.

The same process may be used to manage negative spontaneous feelings about the self that often occur if a person has a developmental history of attachment problems with family, especially the primary attachment figure. Children who experience indifference, neglect or rejection from their attachment figures tend to blame themselves for these difficulties. This appears to be the only choice they may have as blaming parents is conceived as a behavior can generate negative results. Blaming the self usually results in what may be called a negative self meaning a feeling of being bad or unworthy or deserving of negative responses from others. This negative self continuously affects how others responses are viewed. Sometimes this negative self is so prominent that a person constructs a view of social situations so as to behave in ways that result in rejection by others. Often this response by others occurs not because of negative feelings but because of a desire to help an individual feel better but having no idea about how to do this.

This is where *thinking* becomes so important. Remember that the brain stores feelings that arise from emotional experiences, especially those that occur during developmental years. A dysfunctional attachment response on the part of the primary attachment figure or other family attachment figures will be registered in the emotional sector of the brain. These feelings are energized and continually seek expression. For example, a child who has been treated with indifference, neglect or rejection can have feelings of loss associated with those experiences. This can generate a longing within for repairing and restoring that loss. The child part of the personality that continues through adolescence and into adulthood desires to be fulfilled. This often will appear with mild and sometimes more serious depression or sadness that can affect adaptation and social functioning. If one realizes the cause of these feelings and *thinks* analytically about them, they can be controlled. Persistence in *thinking* realistically may result in a permanent resolution of bothersome feelings.

Thinking is a present time behavior. Feelings also may be in the present but often the negative or worrisome feelings associated with indifference, neglect or rejection come from past history. If one *thinks* about this clearly, one can differentiate the child's needs from the adult's present time situation and focus on the moment. Living in the moment and focusing on what you are doing at the moment is an important way to behave. This is mindfulness.

The point here is that *thinking* about negative or worrisome feelings is the type of experience that has the potential to create new neural pathways which replace those associated with difficult emotional experiences from the past. Once this happens the feelings associated with those experiences may disappear. To accomplish this requires considerable attention and focus but it can happen.

Thinking is also important in a crisis in which an obstacle to a life goal appears to be insurmountable using ordinary problem solving strategies. If you encounter a person in crisis help them to define the event that generated it. Introduce the thinking for them by taking leadership in clarification until a balance in their thinking and the organization of problem solving begins. In this situation, you are lending them your strength until their own strength returns.

To justify the importance of *thinking* consider this brief summary of Albert Ellis's *Rational Emotive Therapy*. He proposed that people create their own emotional distress by making illogical assumptions about experiences with assumptions leading to self-defeating ideas and behavior. We upset ourselves by believing that others can upset us and make us feel bad about ourselves. Sometimes these upset feelings can result in a diagnosable psychiatric illness.

Ellis distinguished emotion from *thinking* in that emotion may be based on a biased perception while *thinking* is based primarily on objective fact and reality. *Thinking* will help correct erroneous interpretations of emotional response to experience, make a distinction between inappropriate and appropriate emotions, aid in seeing the difference between rational and irrational *thinking* and promote appropriate emotional responses.

Reality-oriented *thinking* can be learned in the same way anything else is learned. Earlier in the book there was a discussion of mental functions such as memory, judgment, learning, developing relationships, postponing gratification and interpreting reality as it really is. You will discover that *thinking* appropriately about emotions restores balance in the mind to the point where these functions will be more effective.

A middle-aged woman who feels depressed every day is an example. She cried spontaneously. She talked about feeling anxious. That feeling probably is more accurate because, although she is feeling depressed, the reason is that she believes she is ineffective and dysfunctional and everyone around her sees her that way. She is one of those individuals who is both anxious and depressed with the latter being a response to the anxiousness about how she functions and what she thinks people around her feel about her. She did have difficult real life experiences which she believes are her fault. Her behavior is erratic and she medicated her feelings by drinking a lot of beer which led to several DUI convictions. She grew up in a dysfunctional setting and incorporated many negative self feelings and anger. During counseling sessions she learned a new perspective. She recognized that her behavior was self-punishing. With this recognition, she made significant changes in her behavior. She learned to *think* about her very difficult developmental history and the effect it had on making ineffective decisions. She learned to think about her self-blame and realized this was an inappropriate feeling.

Remember, no one experiences total positives during their developmental years. There are always some disappointing events or feelings of discomfort that may create lasting negative emotional imprint. These events require adaptation. The likely outcome can be positive if the energy with which you were endowed and the nature of the relationship with your primary caretaker and family was sufficient.

This chapter dealt with feelings and thinking about which you may learned something about both. You also may have learned that the other's expression of feelings comes from them and should not be personalized or internalized. You also may have developed a different reaction to emotional situations by knowing that feelings are just feelings that are not good or bad, right or wrong and cannot be judged. You may have also learned something about thinking and how it can help develop a new perspective about feelings that were a response to problematic developmental experience.

Chapter 13
Mental Functioning

Sigmund Freud is likely the most widely known theorist about the structure of the mind. He conceptualized the mind as having three parts, ego, superego and id. The ego is both conscious and unconscious of which the conscious is the self-aware part of the personality. The unconscious is where mental defense mechanisms are located. The superego is a collection of rules about learned social behaviors. It also is unconscious except for the conscience that is conscious. This is the part of the mind that lets one know whether a behavior is right or wrong according to the superego rules. The content of the superego is generated by the process of socialization, what one is taught, formally or informally, and what one experiences in the reactions of others about the propriety or impropriety of a behavior. The id is unconscious and the seat of basic drives and instincts that seek pleasure, avoid pain and influence behavior, feelings and thinking. For example, humans are driven by the instinct of self-preservation. Whenever this is threatened anxiety appears followed by a defensive reaction to manage the anxiety.

Freud thought that all the energy of human mental and physical operations was in the id. Through the influence of his daughter and colleagues in his inner circle he changed his beliefs to seeing the ego has its own energy and is not dependent upon the id. This radically changed ideas about counseling or psychotherapy for emotional disorders. Previously these treatment mechanisms were limited to free association in psychoanalysis, dream interpretation and interpretation of slips of the tongue. With the ego having its own energy system direct conversational interchange between a counselor and client became a reality. This made psychotherapy much more available since other professionals were licensed to do psychotherapy.

Thomas Harris wrote about an alternative structure of the mind. In his form, there also are three parts that correspond to Freud's thinking about the ego, id and superego which he labeled adult, child and parent. The adult is the rational, reasonable, thinking and problem solving part of the mind while the child is the demanding, self-oriented, feeling and wanting part. The parent is rule oriented and structured. The adult tries to maintain a balance in the personality by interpreting reality for what it really is. The adult controls the child who desires what it wants immediately while the parent sets and enforces the rules of behavior.

This model is one that has practical uses for self-analysis and self-awareness. You may be able to recognize the child and the parent in yourself and see those times when the child wants something unreasonable or wants an impulsive decision to override a thoughtful one. You may also be able to see when the parent is interfering with reasonable pleasures or setting a thought pattern of guilt when the intended behavior is harmless. Thinking about this clearly may make a significant difference in how you feel and behave.

Neuroscience presents another point of view. Feelings resulting from experiences create what are called neural pathways in the brain. These pathways form neural networks that affect behavior, feeling and thinking and therefore adaptation and social functioning. They are a part of the anatomy of the brain, its physiology or functions. One theory suggests that negative emotional experiences are stored in a part of the brain that governs emotions that, when expressed, may be quite negative. The effect of these negative emotional experiences is consistent and stable but can be changed through new positive experiences. This idea of neural plasticity is one characteristic that makes the brain an amazing organ. This can be demonstrated in the brain's capacity to respond to rehabilitation after a stroke.

No one grows up perfectly normally. Humans are humans with all the problems and challenges that come with being human. We learn a great deal when we are small and the examples that others offer us is stored in memory. Memory has sometimes been likened to an old-style library card catalog with many hundreds of "drawers" and an accompanying index that describes the location in the brain of every experience that has created a memory. Memories are stored in the preconscious mind. Upon occasion a trigger will generate the recall of a memory that hasn't been conscious for some time. This may result in scary feelings especially if the memory is unpleasant.

The important thing to recognize is that memories of everything that has happened to you are stored including unpleasant memories that occasionally enter into consciousness. This recreates an opportunity to rethink the reality of the memory and learn new perspectives which may relieve anxiousness.

A diagnosis of serious psychiatric illness about which people should be aware includes bipolar disorder, major depression and schizophrenia. Since the direct cause of these disorders is not known, a cure is not attainable. A number of professionals believe that traumatic emotional experience during developmental years is often a contributing factor. Mental or emotional illnesses are adaptive mechanisms although they are not effective as such. Recovery from these illnesses, in which the chronic illness is not a major factor in a person's life, is possible. Medical intervention and therapeutic medication along with continuous monitoring by a mental health professional may be necessary.

Psychotherapy or counseling also may be very helpful for recovery. Many persons who suffer from chronic serious psychiatric illness continue to have rational, thoughtful periods in their lives. They are able to engage in talk therapy about traumatic experiences and to reframe them in a way that changes their feelings. It is worthy to note here that many mental health professionals believe psychotherapy is not effective with serious and persistent mental illness. However, there is increasing evidence that this isn't accurate. It is interesting that talk therapy, counseling or psychotherapy can have the same positive effect on brain chemistry as medication. It is generally accepted that the chemistry of the brain is the locus for emotional disorders. It has not, however, been determined whether the deficits in chemistry generate the emotional disorder or if the chemistry of the brain is affected and diminished in its effect by the onset of the disorder itself. However, psychotherapy can affect the brain positively. These results have been measured by new electronic tools that recently have been used by neuroscientists to measure changes in the brain resulting from psychotherapy.

Treatment of serious psychiatric illness presents many challenges requiring a comprehensive, multifaceted approach. An individual who is affected by such a condition can deny it and this can be frustrating for family and friends and to mental health providers. However, this denial may be a coping strategy and may be the highest level of functioning that the person can achieve given the traumatic and disappointing challenges they may have experienced. In this context, it may be better to look at life experiences and whether some change can be made in how a person continues to react to memories of them rather than to focus on a specific diagnosis. In fact, except for a trained physician, psychiatric diagnosis should not be the focus. Rather, the focus in treatment should be on the behavior of adaptation and social functioning without specific reference to the diagnosis.

Treatment for these persons can be very difficult if the illness is denied since there won't be an acceptance of change. Continuing emotional support by family and caregivers with gentle questioning of a person about what is believed about aberrational thinking and behavior is one way to approach this. Patience is required with realistic attention to providing a person's basic needs, especially attention and affection. It is these positive experiences that produce the greatest chance of a change in neural pathways which can lead to better social functioning.

Requiring treatment for a mental condition may have a significant positive outcome. Sometimes legal means including commitment to a psychiatric facility may have to be employed especially in those cases where a person is a danger to her/himself or others. This action can be upsetting for everyone involved since it often generates angry feelings that can be long lasting. However, the safety of both the individual and those who support her or him must come first.

Regular consultation with a qualified psychiatrist is necessary when a person is being treated for serious psychiatric illness. These illnesses are chronic although there are some acute events following which symptoms recede. Adaptation, in which one gets to the point of the illness not being a major factor in one's life, is an objective. Adaptation may be assisted by focusing on normative behavior. For some people exploring developmental experience where indifference, neglect, rejection or trauma occurred may be helpful when the person is able to rethink and relearn appropriate responses to negative emotional events. However, this exploration can sometimes bring to mind overwhelming troubling memories that activate the behavioral symptoms of the illness. If this occurs, immediate medical intervention including hospitalization may be required. If one is actively psychotic, psychotherapy is not recommended until the psychotic episode has ended.

It may be helpful to the reader to consider this brief summary of psychotherapy. When you visit a physician about a physical illness, questions about your physical history are asked as a way to diagnosis and treat the problem. The same is true with a mental health clinician who will ask questions about your developmental history in order to assess the effect of those experiences on your adaptation and social functioning. The purpose is to define the source of the problem and the ways that you have been trying to resolve it. The discussion that follows may create a new understanding of negative developmental events and relief from anxiety about them.

There are mental defense mechanisms that everyone uses to avoid anxiety. If these defenses are working the clinician may choose to support them as they are fulfilling their purpose. However, it should be understood that these defenses don't work well all the time. A mental health professional can help a client gain self-awareness about the effect of emotional experiences that contributed to the problem. Then one can rethink and relearn a new interpretation of these events that may relieve the anxiety without the defenses. This may take several sessions which should be provided by a trained and licensed professional.

Knowledge about neuroscience, especially about neural pathways and neural plasticity, can be very useful. When seeking treatment for an emotional disorder, individuals may want to inquire about whether the clinician knows something about neuroscience. This awareness highlights the contributions of physiological factors to the assessment and treatment of emotional disorders. Awareness of basic neuroscience concepts can make a significant contribution to a clinician's ability to help a client make a better adaptation to emotional and mental disorders. Neuroscience has established the existence of neural pathways in the brain which are generated through experience. These may include those that are related to attachment. It is these pathways within networks in the brain that likely contribute to adaptation and social functioning. Neuroscience also provides evidence of neural plasticity which may underlie the brain's ability to adapt and change in response to the environment including changes brought about by psychotherapy.

Knowledge about neuroscience can be learned, especially about developmental experiences and their effect on forming neural pathways and neural plasticity. Knowing this may make it possible to change these neural pathways with new experiences. Another positive benefit is awareness that dysfunctional behavior and feelings are not one's fault as this is what they learned through experience. This is not to say that one doesn't have a responsibility to change. One can learn that developing new experiences creates new neural pathways which replace the old dysfunctional ones generating new adaptive skills that can lead to positive social functioning and a secure attachment style. Knowing how the brain functions can provide more self-control and perseverance in problem solving. This approach may be easier to accept and understand as the problem they have can be viewed as having a physiological base rather than an emotional one. Encouraging one to think about these ideas and to discuss them with a knowledgeable mental health professional can be very helpful. Reorganizing the thinking of a person with a psychiatric illness is generally more productive.

Case management is a prominent technique used with persons who have a mental illness but who may not be candidates for traditional psychotherapy. The most frequently used is the broker model which consists of assessing basic needs such as shelter, food, clothing and social contacts. Needless to say, considerable skill is required for case management to be successful. Knowledge of community resources is required as a person's needs may extend beyond the clinician or agency resources. Referral skills also may be required as is follow up to make sure a client made contact with the referred source. Many times it is necessary for a clinician to go with the client to the referral location and meet the staff who will be seeing the client. Transfer of the relationship to a new person is important for many clients.

Changes in medical treatment of serious psychiatric illness have occurred through recognizing that most medical practice has been oriented around acute or immediate care which is an approach that doesn't fit the nature of chronic mental or physical illness. Integrated care which includes treatment of all forms of chronic illness, whether mental or physical, by a team of skilled providers in the same setting has recently emerged as a significant process.

Integrated care requires the conceptualization of medical services as a team effort.

Professionals with various education and training in health care are assisted by necessary support staff. Technology plays a significant role as self-monitoring equipment may be employed with automatic messages sent to the integration team for monitoring purposes. The desired outcome is for the patient to self-manage the chronic illness with the assistance of the team so that the illness is not a major factor in the patient's life and recovery occurs This response format to chronic illness has the likely result of a considerable reduction in the stigma associated with mental illness since the mental illness is considered a chronic illness. The chronic illness is treated by the same team of providers. If you or someone close to you is seeking treatment for a mental illness, an integrated care facility may be the best choice as it provides a comprehensive emotional and physical care program.

Neuroscience is the coming field for the assessment and treatment of emotional disorders with numerous technological advances occurring in the last 25 years that have affected mental health therapeutic interventions. One of the most effective of neuroscience concepts is the idea of neuroplasticity which is s basic idea that the brain is an organ capable of change to meet whatever challenges may occur. The brain can adjust itself to new and different experiences and is capable of adapting to practically anything. It can even accommodate damage as the result of a stroke and is capable of learning new things throughout life. The idea of neural plasticity confirms that learning never ends.

The brain has multiple synaptic connections that are involved in its functioning. Neural pathways are a series of these synaptic connections formed with every experience. To get a sense of these synaptic connects in the body simply touch your finger to a spot on your forearm. The message of having been touched travels to the brain instantly. This is impressive considering the power and complexity of the brain, an organ about the size of your fists side by side, with its many synaptic connections. What's even more impressive is that so many potential functions of the brain remain unknown.

It's important to be aware of what neural pathways are and how they are constructed. From the time we are born neural pathways are being created in the brain. Neuroscience research has demonstrated that brain cells form neural networks which communicate with each other. Neural pathways are created with every experience and remain as active influencers on the mind. Recall that the mind and the brain are different. The brain is the anatomical structure or the content so to speak, while the mind is physiological or a process.

Negative emotional experiences impact the brain and are stored in the emotional center. The energy they possess pushes for their expression so they can often interfere with effective adaptation and social functioning. It is important to know that deliberately creating new positive emotional experiences will create a reaction in the brain whereby the old memory traces are replaced. The effect is to increase adaptation and social functioning. Sometimes the assistance of a professional mental health professional is required to achieve this end.

Professional help is readily available either through private health insurance or a public mental health agency. It is important to have information about the history of the mental health system in an effort to use it appropriately. Knowing about the history of the system can help in understanding the effect that it has on current practice including certain factors that have changed the delivery of medical care.

In 1773 when first hospital for the mentally ill opened in the United States, there were very few such care facilities. Clifford Beers, a mentally ill person, wrote the book <u>A Mind That Found Itself</u> which was the beginning of a mental hygiene movement. However, it was 30 years before the federal government established the Division of Mental Hygiene within the US Public Health Service. Partly due to the number of WWII soldiers returning home with serious mental problems, the army neuropsychiatry program called upon the federal government for action leading to the Mental Health Act of 1946 followed by the creation of the National Institutes of Mental Health in 1949.

Following a series of ups and downs in federal funding of programs for the mentally ill, the mid 1980s saw case management established as part of Medicaid and behavioral health became separately funded from physical health benefits. However, federal program funding continued to be problematic until President George W. Bush increased funding for Community Health Centers and formed the New Commission on Mental Health which brought considerable attention to the delivery of mental health care.

In the mid-1990s the Chronic Care Model (CCM) was created by Wagner and his associates. The CCM was designed to modify medical service delivery from an acute to a chronic focus. The elements of the CCM are productive interactions between informed activated clients and a skilled practice team. Activated clients are those who are informed and motivated to manage their own chronic illness and are supported by the skilled practice team. The goal is for the person to self-manage chronic illness as much as possible. The CCM views medical practice, whether large or small, as linked with community resources to enlarge the delivery system so people have access to a broad array of services. Education concerning the use of these services is consistently provided by the skilled practice team. Interventions are planned that focus on the person and family's part in encouraging and sustaining self-management of the illness. While education about the illness is important, creating within the person the self-confidence needed to manage their own chronic illness is more significant. Face-to-face contact between the skilled practice team and the person is not required with telephone calls and group meetings often being used.

A CCM organization must have teams of experts in clinical and behavioral management. This requires leadership to make training resources and internal structures available such as an electronic record keeping system which makes client information readily available to appropriate staff.

Integration of care for mental and physical illnesses is occurring slowly in primary practice. It is suggested that readers become familiar with integration of care since the choice of such a system can provide the most effective service. Note that larger organizations with public funding generally are able to achieve a level of integration which is more difficult for smaller primary practices. However, primary practice is changing as there are fewer small offices with physicians increasingly being employed by hospitals, practice groups, local public organizations and federal health centers. It is in these settings where integration likely will occur although the leadership of the organization has to make it happen.

Be aware that integration within a practice runs the gamut from minimal collaboration between and among the providers to a fully integrated model. A fully integrated system is one site, one reception area, one electronic record, one treatment plan, integrated funding and one board. This is the one to consider if you, or a family member, need mental health care. It is important to consider that many clients with chronic mental illness also have co-occurring chronic physical illness.

Private medical insurance can make it easier to obtain appropriate care. However, for those with high-deductible insurance plans it may be necessary to pay for services until the deductible is met. In many cases there may be a co-pay. Although there may be limitations at the state level, federal parity law requires payments for mental and physical health services when payment conditions are met.

In addition to federal and state assistance, there are local county public resources available. Many large cities have federal health centers that provide services to the poor and low income with some employing the Chronic Care Model. Many provide integrated care at some level and access is usually available 24 hours a day by phone.

The bottom line is that if you or someone you care for needs mental health treatment be sure to get it. Remember that physical pain deserves evaluation and treatment while the pain of emotional distress can be worse and relief certainly is available.

Chapter 14
Relationships

Relationships between and among humans is an essential ingredient in human life. While the need for relationships is a given, there often are problems. This chapter presents a definition of relationships. There is a discussion of good and bad relationships and suggestions of possible ways both can be managed to increase adaptation and social functioning.

Relationship is defined as an attachment to another. Relationship as attachment has a quality that lends itself to some measurement. One can use a measurement of attachment as an indication of the significance of a relationship. These measures are available on the Internet.

Types of human relationships include casual, ethical, familial, interpersonal, intimate and professional. Casual relationships are informal and tend to have less meaning. Ethical relationships typically occur in business although the concept may be extended further to include a professional relationship in which two or more people have shared goals and a shared plan to achieve them. Interpersonal relationships are those that have some attachment quality, while intimate relationships have both emotional and physical characteristics.

Familial relationships occur among family. The relationship with the primary caretaker who took care of you, fed you, held you and provided a sense of comfort is very important. The concept of familial relationship is generally described to include mother, father, brothers and sisters. Sometimes the term includes extended family of aunts, uncles, cousins and their spouses and children. Most often mother is the primary caretaker and the relationship with her is a primary source of the development of a secure attachment style leading to internalization of a positive self. Relationships with a father and with siblings may also directly affect the development of these personality characteristics. Experiences with these persons form neural pathways through which one develops a sense of being accepted by others.

There are many good relationships such as those between a parent and a child, husband and wife, a significant other, a close friend, a relative, a counselor, etc. These good relationships are based on the secure attachment style of the persons involved in the relationship. There is a freedom of exchange of affection and ideas and communication is largely positive. To be sure, disagreements do occur but they are not taken personally. These relationships rarely are disrupted and there is lasting concern and respect for the other.

Maintenance of these relationships requires constant attention as events that occur are unpredictable. People have many casual contacts with others every day and some of these can be frustrating and create tension. For example, many have demanding and difficult jobs that can be frustrating and anger producing which is an example of the frustration-aggression principle. This principle states that aggression of some form generally follows frustration. The aggression often cannot be released directly against the person generating the frustration so a substitute release is sought. Much of the time this substitute is the person with whom one has a close or intimate relationship but can extend to other relationship types as well.

The person in the relationship who receives the frustrating behavior must maintain the objectivity characteristic of a secure attachment style by listening and not reacting until the frustrated person has released the energy of the anger of the frustration. A good relationship will tolerate such a response. Following this release, a discussion of the frustrating situation may clarify ways to manage a similar event in the future. The supportive nature of the relationship will provide strength to the frustrated individual.

Even in good relationships, there will be different points of view about many issues.

Experience is different for individuals and can result in strong attitudes and opinions. This difference also may generate arguments. The direction these arguments take may be the test of the strength of the relationship. Again the objectivity of the persons in the relationship must be maintained by focusing on the facts associated with the difference and using problem solving to arrive at a solution that is mutually agreeable.

The major point in this book is to *think* rather than feel. When thinking is the dominant form of interpersonal exchange, negative feelings recede. The expression of feeling without thinking often leads to a lack of resolution to a relationship problem. Thought given to positive relationships is a way to change problematic neural pathways resulting from experiencing indifference, neglect or rejection during the developmental years.

The ability to form a positive relationship is related to the level of attachment of the child to the primary caretaker. The need to attach is natural with humans employing an attachment behavioral system that is active throughout life. This system is activated whenever there is a threat of separation from the attachment figure, such as would the case when a caretaker is indifferent, neglectful or rejecting. It organizes an adaptive response aimed at restoring the availability of the attachment figure. When that person returns, the system is deactivated. A failure to restore the relationship can lead to anxiousness. Secure adults have internalized an attachment figure that enables them to maintain a normal balance when the attachment figure is unavailable. The ability to self-soothe contributes to this outcome.

Interpersonal and intimate relationships that help individuals grow emotionally feature a group of characteristics. First, being with a person with whom one has a good relationship creates the feeling like no one else is present. The other person is focused, attentive, listens and responds. The exchanges between the two are purposeful and the conversation is meaningful. Each of the persons in the relationship accepts each other as they are. Emotions are controlled and each owns their feelings. There is respect for the other's ability to determine a course for life and a mutual willingness to exchange helpful ideas when such a request is made. There is no moral judgment about behavior although there is a willingness to talk about moral issues if such a need arises. There is a sense of confidentiality that what is said between the two will not be repeated detrimentally to anyone else. These characteristics typify positive familial relationships during a child's developmental years and between adults in both close and intimate relationships.

Marriage calls for an intimate relationship. In the Western world, the idea of falling in love is a goal of many individuals. As individuals fall in love, some report that they also "fell out of love."

Love is a romantic concept which stays in focus in our culture because many role models are inadequate. We become fascinated by Hollywood personalities and the glamour they seem to possess. Sexual stimulation is constantly presented in movies, on the TV, in shows and advertisements and in novels and magazines. Sex is a selling point for many items and contributes to a sense of aura in a relationship. Sexual attraction becomes a necessary ingredient in a love relationship. Sexual attraction can mean that many of the qualities of an individual are hidden especially those that may later become problems in the relationship.

It can be said with safety that a great many marriages occur with two people who are attracted to each other for neurotic reasons, meaning each has emotional needs they feel the other can meet. Neurotic reasons are not a basis for a good intimate relationship. You may have talked with a person who said they were in love and although they didn't like certain qualities or personality traits of this person, they were convinced that they could change her or him after marriage. This is not a good idea. The attachment style a person adopts is longstanding and the belief that one can change another's style is unrealistic. An attachment style can change but when the relationship develops around attraction based on mutual unmet emotional needs, the probability of that change is not great.

At times, relationships can have problems just because of the nature of the relationship.

This may sound strange until you consider the context. The person with whom you have a relationship may be the person you trust enough to vent frustration and anger when issues arise that are frustrating. There may be times when the relationship partner is also experiencing frustration. When this occurs it won't take much to set off aggressive reactions.

There are people who are just negative. They have a negative self and it gets displayed regularly in their interpersonal relationships. You know who those people are so avoid them when you can. If you cannot, then remember if you are sensitive, a reaction may be coming from your hurt inner child and that won't work most of the time. It is important to get to know yourself and your strengths and weaknesses and think about your reactions.

There may be times when a boss, a work associate or someone in authority makes a negative comment to you. The first response can be anger and resentment as these are feelings that manage fear. All of us want to be accepted. When we hear some critical remark or observe negative behavior toward us we feel the fear associated with a lack of acceptance and become defensive. Many are aware of the flight, fight or fantasy defenses. They are very common. Flight means getting away as quickly as possible. Fight leads to a defensive response, either aggressive or assertive while fantasy can mean a retreat into a daydream. Generally these defenses are not successful as they are not part of the group of positive mental functions.

Flight, fight or fantasy is related to the frustration-aggression principle. When frustration occurs it often will be followed by aggression. This principle often is the basis for angry arguments between relationship partners. When the feelings are positive they generally are not frustrating. When they are negative if a person does not think about the source or the condition of the other that might prompt such a statement, it is likely a return negative statement will be made.

This may occur more frequently in marriage relationships because married people are with each other more than they are with others. This calls for the relationship principles of acceptance and non-judgmental attitude. In a marital relationship, a partner needs to listen to the other and not react personally to what is being said. Sometimes a partner needs to express frustration over whatever may be occurring at the time. Ventilation or "venting" is a healthy behavior and the receiving partner has to strive to realize this at all times. However, it is essential that everyone own and admit their feelings. Remember feelings are never right or wrong or good or bad. They're just feelings. It is behavior that can be judged.

Relationships make the world go around. If you grew up in a family where positive relationships were the general rule the chances are that you have a positive view of yourself and others. This doesn't mean that there were no arguments among family members. Rather it means that even though arguments occurred there were no negative effects or grudges held because the underlying feeling of respect for each other was present. Positive attachment among and between family members promotes normative and mature personalities and the ability to disagree without anger or judgment. Arguments about a subject matter are acceptable. Arguments about a person are not acceptable as these arguments often are filled with personal comments that are hurtful.

Communication, therefore, is an important part of any relationship. Often people in a relationship will comment on not communicating effectively with each other. While there may be many reasons for this such as lack of trust, shame about past behaviors, not being truthful as a way of evading undesirable consequences, lack of sufficient attachment to a partner or anger about a partner's behavior.

There is a communication technique that often is successful. It's not easy but it works.

When your partner says something that expresses a feeling or idea listen carefully and then repeat what you believe you heard. This slows down a reaction because it is a thinking strategy rather than feeling. It also is clarifying because it allows each conversant to plan the next sentence. You may be aware of the tendency to think about a reply before the other has finished talking. The result is that people tend to talk past each other without much mutual understanding. Anxious people tend to do this more than others. Try practicing this technique and see if it helps. You may want to read the chapter on Attachment for more information about relationships.

The effect of difficult familial relationships during developmental years often can create adult problems with adaptation and social functioning in the form of an insecure attachment style. However, this doesn't have to occur. One may find a secure base in another through marriage or another intimate relationship. Fortunately, those who had difficult development experiences are often lucky enough to marry a person with a secure attachment style who becomes their secure base. In such cases over time, and generally not too long, the effect can lead to a change in attachment style for the one with developmental attachment difficulties. Continuing this relationship can strengthen the marital relationship. There may be bumps in the road along the way but progress can be made.

An example here may be helpful. This example involves Joe who was raised with parents that had serious conflicts. His father was a stern and rigid person. His mother was weak and passive and quite manipulative. She was working when Joe was born and went back to work about a week after she and the baby came home from the hospital. The father was a farmer and worked outside most of the time leaving the baby in a crib. This separation from the primary attachment figure created a sense of mistrust of both parents. Mother would not or could not answer personal questions about her feelings. Father was a rugged individualist who showed no warmth toward the son. Mother didn't want son to be a farmer so she stood in the way of his learning anything about farming. The relationship with both parents contributed to the son's feelings of inferiority. He had a difficult time making friends in elementary, high school and college and had many psychogenic worries about health. While his functioning was not severely affected, he was often unhappy.

While on a break from the university he met a girl who was in his high school class at a local dance. When he took her home she invited him to come to her house the following Sunday. This started a long term relationship. They were married three years later and have been married for over 60 years. This relationship has been very satisfying and the attachment to his wife has provided security for Joe. Over time he has matured and learned to manage the difficult feelings from his developmental years. He continues to have some psychogenic complaints but because his wife is a nurse she is able to relieve his worries. The relationship has been so supportive that the effects of the troubled developmental experiences have been largely overcome.

This is one of those situations in which relationship has been a positive influence. Along with it has come input from his wife about realistic thinking about self and the interpretation of events. Married partners that work together and have respect for each other even when they disagree have no continuous negative feelings. They work together to solve problems and stand together in the face of adversity.

When you get into a relationship, think about what you are doing. Superficial reasons for attraction to another will disappear rather quickly and after a time, the real personality can appear. Make every effort to see the real person beneath the cover. Just as thinking is important about difficult feelings, it is essential to think clearly about the potential for a significant relationship. People talk about falling in or out of love but most cannot describe what this means. Two people liking each other is the main ingredient of a good relationship. This means the individuals share many mutual interests, an ability to relate appropriately to each other and mutual respect and concern.

Relationships are involved at an individual's work place. They either work in a support role or are involved in the management. Either way, they are directly affected by the organization so spouses and children can also be affected, though indirectly. Both parents may work and the interface of feelings about their respective jobs can be stressful causing strain in that relationship.

There are a variety of issues involved in how one manages time at work and balances that with time spent outside work. Some of these are presented in this chapter since involvement at work may be significant in adaptation and social functioning. The factors are presented serially but not in rank order.

An initial concern is the fit between the worker and the work. The worker brings a set of situational circumstances to the work situation. This includes preparedness for the work such as education and prior work experience. Given that a new worker doesn't know the work situation, the question is how the worker can adapt to the setting and function. Other factors involved include the attitude and personality of the supervisor and the manner in which decisions affecting workers are made. Also important are relationships with fellow workers, the amount of noise or distraction and the working capacity of whatever machine or tools are required for the job. In the case of an office worker or professional, the location of where one spends most of the time can be significant.

Fit between the worker and the work depends largely on the similarity of their values.

These values are enduring on both sides and when different or opposing, the fit of the worker to the organization can be a problem. The culture of the individual also should match the culture of the organization. Culture in this case can be defined as the accepted beliefs, behaviors and values that are passed from one generation to the next. When the values and cultures of each are a close match, it is likely the worker will be more satisfied with the work and the organization more satisfied with the worker. Sometimes tolerance of cultural differences may be required.

Human behavior often is determined by the beliefs and values that are learned through social influences since people learn to be what they are. There is no particular right way to do many things although a right way often determined by the setting in which behavior occurs. Differences about how to do things may generate distress so people who differ may want to be careful about making judgments about others.

The recruitment of a worker often is based on what the recruiter can determine about the worker's values during employment interviews. The more these values are compatible with the values of the organization and the values of the existing work force, the more likely a worker will be hired and be successful. After being hired socialization begins and it is through this process that the worker learns to adapt to the organization's expectations and values in order to maintain social functioning within the organization. Ideally socialization should include organizationally sponsored social events at which senior management are present. Training programs are another way to promote socialization.

For those who are looking for a job or thinking about changing jobs, there are some things to consider. These suggestions may not be appropriate for every worker in every situation. Research whatever information is available about a prospective work place. Talk with workers there. These efforts may lead to a better understanding of the values and culture of the organization. Be aware that determining the reality of the situation can be difficult as some workers will be satisfied and happy at the job while others may be dissatisfied. If possible, one way to discover the reality is to inquire about the possibility of spending some time in the organization with other workers of different status to directly observe the values and culture. Values may be more significant than culture in the beginning because values generally are enduring although socialization into a culture can have the effect of modifying values to improve the fit between the worker and the organization.

Performance of the work of the organization is largely determined by the match between the tasks associated with the work and the knowledge, skills and abilities of the worker. Read and understand the job description carefully and discuss details with the employment interviewer to determine the extent of the fit.

Finally, racism is a significant relationship problem and although positive change has occurred, there is much yet to be accomplished. The details of institutional and program change that are needed is beyond the scope of this book although if those who have power would think about the many issues involved rather than feel in ways that are not helpful things could get better. Positive relationships among all segments of the population could increase the general welfare of all. All people are human beings. Skin color or ethnic background does not alter that quality.

Chapter 15
Examples of *Success* in Thinking

This chapter consists of examples about how the thinking process as described in Chapter 5 was successfully applied. You may want to re-read Chapter 5 very carefully to understand the process so you can try it and see if it works for you. These examples should be read with the understanding that the process can be used by anyone reflecting on their own history of emotional distress.

One can recall the context of difficult emotional incidents in their lives. Sufficient knowledge of attachment theory was provided in Chapter 7 for the explanation phase. Those readers interested in learning more about attachment theory can find information about the theory on the Internet along with data about articles and books written about it. Some articles can be retrieved from the Internet. The content of Chapter 6 was about critical thinking for the thinking phase. Critical thinking is an examination of the reality of the quality of attachment to the primary and secondary attachment figures and the indifferent, neglectful and rejecting experiences by these figures or significant others that occurred during child and adolescent years.

These are stories that could apply to anyone. If a reader sees herself or himself in any of them, it is purely coincidental. The purpose of reading these stories is to learn about how the model works. As you read them what appears to be a common thread in all of them? How do you relate to what you learned about the person? Have you had similar experiences? If you have, what did you try to do? Does the process of context, explanation and thinking make sense to you? Have you tried it? If you did what was the result?

The first story is about Marion. His main problem was his anxiousness about himself. The *context* of his early life was difficult. He is preoccupied with rejection. He worries about what others feel about him so he lives an isolated life. He is able to function normatively except when some rejecting incident triggers his anxiety. He has brothers and sisters but he doesn't relate well with them. His relationship with his parents is strained. He visits them occasionally but usually is uncomfortable. He was much closer to his mother than his father. He reported that he has a sense of not being good enough or capable. He feels negative about himself and believes that others can see that in him. He avoids social interaction. As a result he generally experiences a lot of anxiousness. His lack of masculine identity is troublesome to him.

Marion's lack of attachment to his family was the focus of the *explanation* phase. He recalled the distinct differences between himself and his brothers. He identified more with his mother so the feminine side of his personality was more pronounced. However, this made him uncomfortable. The relationship was strained. He felt more rejected than protected.

Marion understood how these circumstances affected his confusion about himself. During the *thinking* phase he was able to connect his angry feelings with the circumstances. As he thought more about this he also began to realize that his view of others' negative attitude toward him resulted from his not liking himself. It also explained his angry reaction as he was interpreting this as rejection and was angry as a way of managing his fear.

It took time for Marion to *think* clearly about his reactions. This is because the confusion and perceived rejection occurred very early in his life and left a strong imprint on his memory. He often accepted intellectually the reality of the effect of negative developmental experience but found it difficult to accept it emotionally.

Emotional acceptance occurred after further *explanation*. Marion became more aware of the effect of lack of attachment to his family. He also became aware that he is vulnerable to perceiving rejection even when it isn't occurring. Thinking more clearly Marion was able to acknowledge that with some exceptions he behaved like a person with an insecure attachment style. This helped him to see his dysfunctional feelings and *think* more about what he had to change. Continuing *thinking* resulted in behavior change. The combination of knowing what behavior had to change and *thinking* about how to do it became the platform for his moving from an insecure style to a secure one.

Another story concerns Frank. The *context* of his developmental history was difficult. His parents separated when he was very young.

His mother was not very stable mentally. As a child he was her primary support system. His father was an alcoholic who didn't offer a positive relationship. As a teen, Frank got a job and an apartment and functioned fairly well. He married but divorced a few years later. He married again and his wife asked for marriage counseling as Frank's behavior had become quite angry with her children.

Explanation involved learning about attachment theory and how the lack of attachment to either of his parents affected his self-esteem. He considered his feelings of loneliness and anger. He came to understand the connection between his negative feelings and thoughts as self-blame for his parents' failures. *Thinking* clearly about these feelings made a difference as his functioning with his wife and step-children improved.

Frank's spontaneous negative feelings continued but were diminished. Through *thinking* about their origination he was able to control his reaction to them most of the time by thinking that he learned negative self-feelings as a child and blamed himself for perceived failures when neglect and rejection were the real causes. He recognized that his feelings followed his experiences. His wife was very supportive. She reminded him about the importance of *thinking* about his feelings. She genuinely cared for him. Her secure attachment style helped him to become more secure. His progress continued and his behavior stabilized at a normative level.

The next story is about Ruth. Ruth came for counseling to find out why she was feeling both anxious and depressed. She works at a manual job often with overtime hours. She is divorced and has two sons. Her ex-husband was not regularly employed during her marriage so Ruth was responsible for supporting the family.

The context of her developmental years was difficult. Her father was an alcoholic. Her parents' relationship was not congenial. She remembers her mother as always having been attentive and good to her. However, she couldn't remember a time when she didn't feel inadequate. Kids picked on her in school so she felt isolated. She attended a religious based school and remembered continually feeling guilty. She married in her late teens. The marriage never was happy and ended in divorce.

It was clear that her early developmental history was difficult although Ruth suppressed these memories. However, the impact was a feeling of inadequacy from which she had not recovered. While talking about this period in her life Ruth said she could understand the possibility of a shortfall of attachment to her mother because of her mother's problems in coping with her father's alcoholism. This led to the *explanation* phase of thinking when she recalled that her three brothers picked on her constantly during her developmental years. Her mother did not prevent this and Ruth could see that insufficient attachment to her alcoholic father and her brothers as secondary attachment figures probably was responsible for her feelings of inadequacy. Being picked on by school mates reinforced those feelings.

The concept of working models was explained to Ruth. From this understanding she knew why she felt uneasy in interpersonal relationships. She asked for more discussion of this concept. Ruth began to understand how important attachment feelings are and how negative working models affected her perceptions of self and others. As her understanding increased she gained a positive perspective and felt better about herself.

During the *thinking* phase Ruth was helped to understand the challenges she faced as a child and early adolescent. She was also able to see that none of the difficult things that occurred were her fault. Realistic *thinking* about her developmental issues and how changing her working models could help made it easier for her to talk about current problems. Her ex-husband was not in good health during and after their marriage. He died a few years after the divorce. Ruth then met a man with whom she had a common interest. This common interest brought them together frequently leading to a more intimate relationship. This turned out to be a problem as the boyfriend never indicated an interest in a permanent commitment. Ruth felt as if he was just using her for sex. However, her need for an attachment kept her involved. Further sessions with Ruth lead to her gaining more self-awareness about why she felt inadequate and unhappy. She formed a strong attachment relationship with her counselor and her self-esteem increased considerably. She withdrew from the intimate part of her relationship although continuing the common interest contacts. She evidenced more and more ability to *think* clearly about her behavior and what she wants out of life. She is much happier and feels more energetic. She no longer is anxious or depressed.

Another story is about Gloria. She was very unhappy and abused alcohol to manage her unhappiness. The *context* of her life was filled with rejection that occurred when she was very young. Her parents never married. Her father wasn't part of her life. Her mother was preoccupied with surviving and didn't pay a lot of attention to Gloria and often was openly rejecting telling her she was no good and would never amount to anything. Gloria didn't do well in school but managed to graduate from high school.

At the suggestion of a friend Gloria began attending Alcoholics Anonymous meetings. This made a difference as she found the meetings to be helpful. She sought explanation for her drinking and began to read materials about attachment theory that was suggested by an AA member. During *explanation*, Gloria recognized her feeling of self-blame and guilt that came from not having a significant positive attachment to her mother. She realized she had developed a negative self. She was able to think about how and what she could do to change her erroneous assumptions about herself. *Thinking* about the error of these assumptions generated sufficient change for her adaptation and social functioning to become normative. She achieved and maintained sobriety. This improvement continued.

The last story is about Tom. Tom is receiving disability compensation. A reason for seeing a counselor was to obtain a mental evaluation for his disability agency. He walks with a cane and has limited mobility. He has an employment related injury. He had spinal surgery that he said did not work and goes to a pain clinic regularly but isn't getting any relief.

Tom is mildly depressed. He had a good paying job before the back injury and feels inferior because he cannot work and support his family. His wife works still the family had continuing financial problems. He receives Medicaid assistance. Tom's depression is chronic. It doesn't improve because his social situation has little prospect of change. Tom is discouraged and sometimes feels like just giving up.

An assessment was completed and submitted a report to the disability agency. Tom decided to continue counseling for his depression. His *context* was positive for difficult attachment experience. His parents divorced when he was young. He doesn't remember his father. His mother married again and his stepfather was negative and punitive. He remembered a lot about his early life and that he always felt unhappy. He had a limited attachment to his mother. His relationship with his stepfather was unfulfilling so he had no role model. He got along fairly well with his brothers but felt they were more successful. Elementary school mates were not friendly. He graduated from high school and left home to take a job as an over-the-road truck driver. He met and eventually married a woman who became his co-driver. They are still together. They have a child for whom Tom provides most of the care because his wife works. The little girl is very intelligent. Tom gives her a lot of attention and teaches her many things that aid her advancement.

After gathering data about Tom's development history for *context*, the *explanation* phase began. Tom recognized that many unfortunate incidents occurred around him during his developmental years, especially the unresponsive attitude of his father, his limited attachment to his mother, the unfriendly response of his school mates and the perception that his brothers were more successful than he. These resulted in his feeling unhappy about life generally. He had never felt attached to anyone until he married. What he did not recognize was that he had internalized a negative sense of himself that affected his motivation to do something to improve his situation.

The *thinking* phase took more time than usual. Tom's chronic depression was difficult to break because of his persistent back pain. This disability reinforced his perception that things were never going to change. Correcting this self-defeating attitude was the main goal of counseling. His self-esteem needed to be improved to the point where he could take some steps to improve his situation.

Several sessions were spent encouraging Tom to rethink his perspective on life, especially to recognize that although he felt rejected by others that what was happening in his environment was creating a lot of stress for everybody in his family. His reaction to a lack of fulfilling attachment was to blame himself even though none of it was his fault. Over time Tom developed an attachment relationship with the counselor. His trust in the counselor increased his motivation to change.

The question of how much Tom's back pain was related to his depression was discussed with his accepting this possibility. He was referred to a rehabilitation center where he was put on a program that after about six months was helpful. They assessed that depression was contributing to the pain. This reinforced the counselor's assessment. This awareness resulted in Tom's rethinking his self-assessment and his self-esteem began to improve. Continued sessions supported his increasing self-esteem. His wife obtained a higher paying job so their financial situation improved considerably. This further decreased Tom's depression and his back pain decreased as well. After a few more sessions a mutual decision was made to terminate counseling. During a follow-up telephone call eight months later Tom said he got a part-time job and everything was going well.

These stories demonstrate the success of this process of *thinking* rather than permitting feelings to influence behavior. One can use this process to develop better self-understanding that will increase adaptation and social functioning.

Chapter 16
It's Not Your Fault

There are many people who suffer from burdening feelings of guilt over issues for which they never had any responsibility. Anxiety and depression may follow strong feelings of guilt. This chapter encourages thinking about how these feelings impact individuals and how relief from them may make a difference in social functioning. What you will learn is that *it's not your fault.*

Guilt feelings arise from having done something wrong as decided by the conscience. Sometimes this is a realistic reflection on an actual behavior. Criterion for realistic guilt is a realization before the behavior that it is wrong followed by a decision to do it anyway. Applying these criteria many behaviors will result in a lack of guilt because criteria were not met. Why then is there such a prevalence of guilt feelings among so many individuals? The answer may lie in having made erroneous assumptions about your responsibility for indifferent, neglectful or rejecting experiences that occurred earlier in your life. Often accompanying these feelings is a sense of badness, unworthiness and self-recrimination. The internalization of a negative self becomes a constant in the behavioral repertoire that can generate various forms of anxiety or depression or both even though what happened was not your fault.

Everyone feels anxious at times. It's a normal emotion. For example, you may feel nervous when faced with a problem at work, before taking a test, or before making an important decision. However, an anxiety disorder is different in that the individual is continuously worried or fearful. The reason for these feelings often is not clear.

When this condition appears one should consider what the cause might be. Since the loss of self-esteem is prominent one question is why is the loss present? It is generally accepted that self-esteem is established through receiving positive, reassuring and nurturing messages from primary and secondary attachment figures. Mother, father and sisters and brothers are these figures in most cases.

Incidents that result in separation from these figures, especially mother, often lead to feelings of self-blame. When these feelings are internalized they affect behavior. Withdrawal from social contacts and the perception of others' negative attitudes toward the self may reach levels at which social functioning is limited because of depression or anxiety. Self-blame occurs even though any separation was not a young person's fault.

There are types of anxiety that may occur because of feeling self-blame such as generalized anxiety disorder, panic disorder, phobias, obsessive compulsive disorder and social anxiety disorder. Generalized anxiety disorder is characterized by a constant fear of impending doom. Panic disorder is a sudden episode of intense fear usually accompanied by physical reactions such as a breathing problem or feeling like one is having a heart attack. Phobias are an extreme or irrational fear of something such as flying or taking an elevator. An obsessive-compulsive disorder consists of recurring unwanted thoughts usually accompanied by repetitive behavior. Social anxiety disorder, sometimes called agoraphobia, is a fear of social contacts that often leaves people confined to their home. It's too bad that so much emotional pain evolves from incidents that were not a person's fault.

Anxiety reactions begin more often during development years when attachment to a primary and secondary attachment figures is so important. A feeling of separation and loss may occur. It may be a physical separation due to the attachment figure's death or illness that interferes with attachment. It also may occur because of the primary attachment figure's negative attitude toward a child. She may not have been ready for a pregnancy, or may not be married or financial circumstances were difficult. This emotional separation has the same effect on the child as a physical separation. The main ingredient is the lack of opportunity for attachment that every child needs. The point here is that whatever the reason it's not your fault.

One may ask about a father's position in the family constellation. Fathers are responsible to care and provide for the mother in every way that generates and sustains her energy that enables her to care for the children. There are some families in which the father is the primary attachment figure. This may occur when the mother is unable or unavailable to fill that position.

One situation that contributes to separation is continuing problems in the parents' marital relationship. When there are a lot of arguments and hostile exchanges between mother and father children become concerned. They may develop a sense of responsibility to do something to help or they may believe they are the cause of the problem. If self-blame occurs guilt and anxiousness will follow. If they believe they should do something to help a feeling of frustration will develop as nothing will seem to work to bring relief. If they believe they failed to resolve the conflict guilt and anxiousness also will occur along with a feeling of emotional distance from the parents.

Either feelings of failing to help or self-blame may result in a negation of self and a feeling of being at fault. When these feelings are internalized problems in developing and sustaining positive interpersonal relationships will diminish. Strong suspicions about the feelings of others toward the self can occur. This can result in withdrawal from social contacts and loneliness. These behaviors in children may be noticed by parents but nothing is done as the parents are so involved in their own distress that they don't reflect adequately on how their conflicts are affecting their children. Elementary school teachers often notice a child's distress but don't do anything unless the child's behavior upsets the classroom learning environment.

This is a time when some children are assessed as having Attention Deficit Hyperactivity Disorder (ADHD). When parents hear this assessment they often consult a physician who prescribes medication for ADHD when the real problem is anxiety. These children should be seen by a mental health professional for an accurate diagnosis and treatment. This process should include a thorough examination of attachment as for many children this will be the problem.

There are some serious problems that can result from indifferent, neglectful or rejecting experiences during developmental years. Children who blame themselves for such experiences may develop anger bordering on rage. This is a defensive reaction to the fear that accompanies indifference, neglect and rejection. These feelings are boiling inside, so to speak, and generate dysfunctional behavior. These children have difficulty making friends, don't do very well with school work, become socially isolated usually by staying in their bedroom. They often are disruptive in school and at home. The internal anger manifests itself in various ways. Some children lose control over their anger and act out violently. This behavior is potentially very dangerous as seen in the school shootings that occur. If you know or are aware of a child or adolescent who might fit this picture do something about it.

It may seem strange to read this but the problem behavior is not their fault. They are acting on distressed feelings and not thinking. Anxiety diminishes thinking and judgment. The ordinary control available to people who are not anxious doesn't operate well in people who are anxious. This is one reason why punishment doesn't help. Punishment will be observed by many children as further indifference, neglect or rejection.

It's appropriate to clarify what is meant by "it's not your fault." Children are very vulnerable in family relationships, especially with a primary caretaker. They are very needy in early years. They are dependent on someone else for food, clothing, shelter and warmth. When treated indifferently, neglectfully, are rejected or sexually abused they learn the world around them, although very limited in scope, is not caring and welcoming. They learn fast as their developing minds soak up everything to which they are exposed. Experience is recorded in the brain. When the experience is mostly negative defenses form to handle feelings. You've probably heard of fight, flight and fantasy as defenses. Children fight by being stubborn, resisting affection, crying a lot and demanding attention. Flight is characterized by withdrawal and a negative twinge when touched or held. Fantasy is observed in daydreaming during which children imagine taking some pleasant or powerful role.

Depression is a mood disorder. It affects a person's thoughts, behavior, feelings, and sense of well-being. It may be a normal temporary reaction to life events such as loss of a loved one or a symptom of some physical illnesses or a side effect of some drugs. The types of depression are: major depressive disorder (clinical depression), persistent depressive disorder (dysthymia), bipolar disorder, seasonal affective disorder (SAD), psychotic depression, peripartum (postpartum) depression, premenstrual dysphoric disorder (PMDD) and situational depressive disorder.

Major depressive disorder (clinical depression) is a serious mood disorder. It causes severe symptoms that affect how you feel, think, and manage daily activities, such as sleeping, eating, or working. A diagnosis of depression requires symptoms such as significant changes in appetite and sleep patterns, irritability, anger, worry, agitation, anxiety, pessimism, indifference, loss of energy, persistent lethargy, feelings of guilt or worthlessness, inability to concentrate, indecisiveness , inability to take pleasure in former interests, social withdrawal, unexplained aches and pains and recurring thoughts of death or suicide. Symptoms must be present for at least two weeks. Not all of the foregoing must be present for this diagnosis.

Persistent depressive disorder (also called dysthymia) is a depressed mood that lasts for at least two years. This person may have episodes of major depression with periods of less severe symptoms.

Bipolar disorder is different from depression. It is listed because a person with this disorder has episodes of extremely low moods that meet the criteria for major depression.

They also have extreme high moods called "mania" or a less severe form called "hypomania."

Seasonal affective disorder (SAD) often occurs annually and is characterized by depression during the winter months when there is less natural sunlight. It may be accompanied by social withdrawal, increased sleep and weight gain and generally goes away during the spring and summer months.

Psychotic depression occurs when a person has severe depression plus some form of psychosis, such as false beliefs (delusions) or hearing or seeing upsetting things that others cannot hear or see (hallucinations).

Perinatal depression is an illness that women experience after giving birth. Women with perinatal depression experience full-blown major depression during pregnancy or postpartum depression after delivery. The feelings of extreme sadness, anxiety and exhaustion that accompany this depressive state may make it difficult for these mothers to complete daily care activities for themselves and/ their babies.

Premenstrual dysphoric disorder (PMDD) consists of affective, behavioral and somatic symptoms that recur monthly during the menstrual cycle.

Situational depressive disorder is short-term depression following traumatic changes in normal life such as divorce, retirement, loss of a job or death of a relative or close friend. It is sometimes labeled adjustment disorder.

Anxiety and depression may occur simultaneously in a person. Even though they occur together they are more appropriately treated as separate entities. In cases where they occur together the depression aspect generally is the most prominent.

Major contributions to anxiety and depression are how one perceives an event and the feelings that occur afterwards. Often people will make erroneous assumptions about their involvement in the event and blame themselves for negative outcomes even though it wasn't their fault. Explaining to these persons that it wasn't their fault may bring relief from anxiety or depression.

Anxiety and depression are emotional reactions to perceptions of events. It's how one interprets what is perceived so it is a follow-up to the event and not a memory of the event itself. These events are almost always related to indifferent, neglecting or rejecting comments or behavior by another who is a significant person in one's life. Children are vulnerable to these reactions by the primary attachment figure (mother) or secondary attachment figures (father and brothers and sisters). They will often blame themselves for the actions of others. Indifferent, neglectful and rejecting experiences may come from other children, either playmates or students. These can have major effects on perceptions of self. If they occur during adolescence, when a young person is struggling to achieve identity, meaning feeling good about themselves and that they fit in the world, the effect can be quite damaging.

A problem is the perception of the self as being flawed when the flaw lies in the other persons, whether parents, friends or acquaintances. That is why *"it's not your fault."* Becoming convinced of this will bring about a much more positive sense of self. It also will clarify that one needs to be very cautious about how some emotional experiences can lead to erroneous perceptions.

Chapter 17
Getting What You Want Out of Life

The suggested variables regarding getting what one wants out of life are presented serially but not in rank order. They are values, the expression of which is attitudes, so they are observable by others.

A beginning idea about this topic is having a positive purpose in life as this provides goal directed behavior. Deciding on achievable goals is important and something to which people fail to give much thought. Many children are taught to go along with whatever is prescribed for them and often punished if they don't. If one does not have goals and some plan to achieve them, life will push one along whatever path external forces provide. There really is no particular purpose to this existence. Over time people fall into a routine that becomes a habit. This can, and often does, result in discouragement and unhappiness and sometimes depression. Therefore thinking about what one really wants to do and setting achievable goals and a plan will give a person a sense of purpose.

Purpose is a reason why something is done. There are many purposes for behavior. Without purpose behavior has no meaning. Purposes that affect what one wants out of life may be observed in personal characteristics such as honesty, respect, truthfulness, faith, hopefulness and charity. There are other personal qualities but a discussion of these will be sufficient for a reader to understand how they relate to getting what you want out of life. It is not expected that these qualities will be fully developed in individuals.

Honesty refers to moral character and attributes such as integrity (another word for honesty), truthfulness and straight forwardness. Can you imagine what it would be like if everyone you encountered demonstrated integrity and truthfulness? Relationships at every level would be enhanced. It is important to temper honesty with kindness as being honest with negative remarks is not well advised.

What would it be like if all the leaders of nations demonstrated integrity and truthfulness? How would that affect international relations? These questions highlight the significance of honesty and integrity as qualities among people that would contribute to everyone getting more out of life.

Respect is a feeling of esteem for someone or something. There are many situations where respect is involved but for the present purpose it is related to interpersonal relationships. It involves the idea of worth. There are too many people whose sense of worth has been diminished by how they have been treated by others, sometimes by parents or persons who have some authority. This invariably results in a decreased sense of self that often is followed by anger and resentment. These feelings sometimes are acted out in behaviorally dangerous ways especially by adolescents or adults who have amassed a huge amount of anger over having been treated indifferently, neglectfully or rejected. Respect is a value that is expressed in attitudes toward others. It appears frequently in an attitude to those who are different from mainstream such as the elderly or youth, the handicapped, the mentally ill, criminals or those who differ in race, ethnicity and culture. All one needs to deserve worth and respect is to be *alive*. Think about how much having respect for life would enhance getting more out of it. Also recognize how many people who are devalued by a society because of their social position would be freed from the burden of feeling as outcasts.

Faith is trust or confidence in someone. Positive relationships are based on faith and develop in children very early in life. The reader may recall the initial psychosocial crisis in Erikson's stage development theory is trust vs. mistrust. The lack of resolution of this crisis has a longstanding effect as it interferes with the resolution of the psychosocial crises of subsequent developmental stages. Faith, therefore, is an important factor in relationships.

Truthfulness means telling the truth. There are many situations in which this is difficult. Parents should encourage children to tell the truth without fear of being punished. Look on children's erroneous behavior as immature judgment and treat each incident as an opportunity for instruction about appropriate behavior. This response will strengthen the attachment bond and the effect may last a lifetime. The old adage "the truth will set you free" is a good guide for anyone. It may be a significant characteristic of getting what you want out of life.

A positive mental attitude is another ingredient of getting what you want out of life. Sometimes we see others who seem to go through life with never a worry or care but what you see isn't what is really happening. No one lives in a totally normative situation. Things go wrong. A parent gets overly angry. People get sick. There's not enough money to pay the bills. Mom and dad argue and scare the kids. The only car breaks down and on and on. These things are impersonal but for some there are more serious issues involving indifference, neglect and rejection during developmental years. For some people life can become a challenge. Maintaining a positive attitude can help facing challenges. Accept the fact that many things cannot be changed or controlled and that bad things happen to good people.

What you want to get out of life often depends on how your life begins. Referring again to Erikson's developmental stages, if one doesn't learn to trust early on, the hope for a successful life is diminished. If one doesn't learn autonomy there may be a sense of shame that may diminish the will. Positive outcomes of stage crises results in hope, will, purpose, competence, fidelity and love.

Hope is the belief that one can obtain what one desires. There are many people who have little hope. Unfortunately, our culture is preoccupied with promoting competition rather than cooperation. Competitiveness pushes people to feel a sense of inadequacy if they don't have the best material goods. This drive appears in education where an "A" is the only acceptable grade. Not being graded at that level frequently incurs anger that is readily apparent in our culture. An example is road rage. Anger can be very destructive and can decrease the sense of hope.

The point is how are we reacting to each other? In our families are we encouraging children to have hope or is a picture of the evilness of the world being presented to the level of discouragement? Are we reacting mostly with feelings rather than thinking carefully about how to react and what to say when negative stimuli appear? The answers to these questions relate to getting what you want out of life because you are contributing to the welfare of others.

Will, the appropriate exercise of choice, is strengthened by the resolution of Erikson's second stage crisis. Withdrawing is the negative outcome. It is apparent that without hope the will is weakened. A sense of shame can be overwhelming at times. For many people there is a need for a supportive environment or assistance in moving from a devalued social position to a valued one.

The point here is the need for a self examination of our social position or status: ascribed versus achieved. An ascribed status is a position that one is born into or has no control over. This is different from achieved status which a person earns based on choice and effort. Examples of ascribed status include gender, eye color, race, and ethnicity. Examples of achieved status are banker, lawyer and physician. In many social positions there are opportunities for kindness and caring that includes people and provides a supportive environment for getting what you want out of life.

It's a good idea to take time periodically to reflect on one's various social positions to learn whether one is moving realistically toward the desired goals. This provides an opportunity for a review of accomplishments and strengths. It may be a time for reevaluating performance and goals and setting new directions when indicated.

With a sense of will comes a sense of purpose that was presented earlier as a significant value for getting what you want out of life. The absence of guilt that characterizes initiative contributes to developing a sense of purpose. Competence, the quality of the Erikson's Industry stage, is a sense of mastery of the environment. This enhances purpose and contributes to achieving established goals.

Identity, which comes from resolution of previous stage psychosocial crises in Erikson's view, is a sense of comfort with oneself and the capacity to relate to others in a manner that contributes to everyone involved in achieving goals. Identity is the platform for resolving the psychosocial stages of adulthood in which the capacity to love and care for others with active concern are individual qualities.

There are many individuals who have problems with identity. The pathological outcomes of lack of resolution of this psychosocial crisis are prominent in negative self-assessment. Questioning people about primary caretakers or attachment figures relationships nearly always leads to relating memories of disappointing, and quite frequently traumatic, experiences with one or both parents. The invariable result is the internalization of self-blame. There is a long lasting feeling of guilt that has never been understood.

The occurrence of indifference, neglect and/or rejection during childhood creates a something of a conundrum. Searching for a reason for the caretaker's behavior, a child realizes that blaming a parent will make the situation worse. Self-blame and guilt likely will be the result.

Immediate relief occurs when a person understands the context of the relationship through a review of parental behaviors and is reassured that what transpired was not their fault. Relearning and rethinking the effect of feelings results in a more positive self-awareness and improved adaptation and social functioning as well as getting what one wants out of life. This process is the main point of this book. You are what you feel but if you *think* it can get better. The strengths one possesses have a lot to do with whether recovery from the emotional distress associated with developmental issues can become a reality. Some of the strengths that contribute to the successful management of losses related to unresolved psychosocial developmental stages are presented. The conscious awareness of strengths promotes clearer thinking about negative self feelings. This is a pathway to relearning about inappropriate feelings that will lead to improved adaptation and social functioning and getting what you want out of life.

Strengths are discussed serially but not in rank order. *Intelligence* is a strength. The more intelligent one is the better their capacity for clear thinking about developmental experiences and their affects. Thinking rather than feeling requires an ability to differentiate between them. Feelings as responses to both positive and negative emotional experiences during developmental years create neural pathways that are stored in the brain. These feelings continue to seek expression. When these experiences and the feelings associated with them have been negative a prevailing assumption is self-blame. The anxiousness, and sometimes depression, that accompanies these assumptions interferes with adaptation and social functioning. Thinking about one's strengths helps in the effort to manage whatever negative self content might be present. That promotes a pathway to getting what you want out of life.

A positive self is a strength that is learned through experience with primary caretakers or attachment figures. There always are flaws in these relationships so the positive is not perfect. The sense that one has worth and the capacity to work toward realistic goals characterizes having a positive self. These people are free of negative thoughts about themselves.

Self-awareness is strength. Those who are realistically able to assess how they function, admit weaknesses and make necessary corrections in behavior will function better. Periodic self-reflection on how one is fulfilling those behaviors of their various social positions helps setting direction for appropriate goals. Knowledge of the impact of developmental experiences on personality increases self-awareness.

Education is strength. The more education one has tends to increase effective adaptation and social functioning because the breadth of knowledge enables one to perceive details and reality more efficiently. At least a high school completion is advised to begin climbing the ladder of success.

Accomplishments are strengths. It is helpful to examine what one has achieved, what skills are involved and what contributions have been made to whatever causes were benefitted. Work is especially important in this regard. Whatever work one does is meaningful and fits into the broad scheme of things. Many people don't reflect on these activities as strengths when if they did it likely would result in a more positive self.

Perseverance is strength. Obstacles may occur to achieving a desired goal. Continuing with whatever is necessary to achieve that goal is the only way. For example, if you haven't been able to graduate from high school and you plan to apply for work that requires a high school diploma you can get a GED (General Education Development) in almost every school district.

Relationships are strengths if they are positive and helpful, characteristics of an attachment relationship that had led to a secure attachment style. Choosing a relationship often relates to one's sense of a positive self that results from successful resolution of the psychosocial crises of each developmental stage. These people have a sense of trust, autonomy, initiative, industry and identity. These qualities enable one to select persons for a relationship that also have successfully resolved the psychosocial crisis of each stage. They promote the ability to get what you want out of life.

A stable marriage is strength. Such a marriage is characterized by husband and wife working together to set and achieve goals. There may be disagreement but these are discussed and negotiated until a mutual decision is made. Sometimes in the heat of arguing comments may get personal but when the argument is concluded there are no bad feelings or grudges. The relationship is stable over time. These two like each other.

Caring is a significant strength in any relationship. It means displaying kindness and concern for others. Caring is particularly important in family relationships especially between husband and wife. Caring is a bond between parents that is observed by children. The outcome for them is they will be caring too.

This chapter has presented ideas about what one might consider are important in getting what you want out of life. The content is not exhaustive as others may have many additional proposals on this topic.

Chapter 18
Crisis Intervention and Trauma

Crises of various types create situations for which an appropriate adaptation depends on the actions of a support person. The individual's ability to think is weakened during crisis so a support person takes responsibility for decisions until thinking capacity is restored.

A crisis exists when a person faces an obstacle to an important goal that cannot be reached through an ordinary problem solving method. Anxiousness is at a high level so ego functions, especially reality testing, judgment and thought processes will be impaired. This is why a support person is important to help compensate for these temporary weaknesses.

During a crisis there is an inner tension, anxiety, disorganization of functions and an extended period of emotional upset. A crisis usually is resolved within four to six weeks whether or not there is professional intervention. Intervention primarily is for the purpose of the person in crisis achieving an improved sense of balance in mental operations. This is brought about by adaptive behavior that solves the conflict and reduces anxiety. Assessment of the ability to resolve the crisis is seen in the individual's capacity to manage anxiety and stress, ability to test reality accurately for problem solving and effective coping mechanisms.

A crisis is likely to occur in response to an event that results in disequilibrium. There are stages to the onset of a crisis: initial response to an external event; inability to engage in effective problem solving and increased anxiousness that drives the person to seek other ways to solve the problem. If these don't work a crisis is reached. The stages in the crisis are: hazardous event, vulnerable state, precipitating crisis, active disequilibrium and reorganization of self functions.

Although many individuals will resolve a crisis without professional help it is important for an observer to recognize when another is in crisis. What this means is that the support person makes decisions and provides direction for action until the person experiencing the crisis regains the ability to manage on their own. It is critical that the support person recognize the point at which the person is able to think clearly enough to do so. Timely withdrawal of support is critical. Empathy is a significant feature of support. A person in crisis may be overwhelmed with emotion. At such times most people are very receptive to the care and understanding of a support person.

The ability to adapt to the emotional demands of a crisis may resolve it, in which case anxiety is reduced and social functioning is restored. If one does not adapt psycho-physiological problems such as headaches, stomach aches or other physical reactions may occur. Behavior may be more immature. These may require professional intervention.

Assistance in a crisis, whether provided by a support person or a professional, is active and directive. The goals of intervention are: return the individual to a previous state of emotional balance or equilibrium; assist the individual to examine the crisis event and think about it in a clear analytical way; and changes in behavior that aid in resolution. *Thinking* rather than feeling, as recommended throughout this book, is essential in crisis resolution.

The crisis intervention guidelines used are the same for all crisis events. The helping person takes over decision making for the person in crisis until the anxiousness of the event diminishes to the point where self-control is regained that supports realistic thinking and problem solving.

Trauma may have a longer term effect than a crisis. The difference between crisis and trauma is that a crisis is a crucial or decisive point or situation, while trauma is any serious emotional or physical injury, often resulting from violence or an accident. Traumatic experiences often involve a threat to life. However, any situation that leaves you feeling overwhelmed can be traumatic, even if it doesn't involve physical harm. It's not the objective facts that determine whether an event is traumatic, but your subjective emotional experience. The more frightened and helpless you feel, the more likely you are to be traumatized.

Emotional and psychological trauma can be caused by events such as an accident, injury, natural disaster, violent attack or relentless stress such as fighting a life-threatening illness. Other causes include surgery, especially in the first three years of life, the sudden death of someone close or a deeply disappointing experience. Experiencing trauma, such as physical or sexual abuse in childhood can have a severe and long-lasting effect. When childhood trauma is not resolved, a sense of fear and helplessness carries over into adulthood, setting the stage for further trauma.

One's responses to trauma are generally expected reactions to abnormal events. Psychological symptoms of trauma are denial, confusion, anger, anxiety, guilt, withdrawal and sadness. Physical symptoms are insomnia, fast heartbeat, fatigue, aches and pains, startle reaction and agitation. Symptoms typically last from a few days to a few months and gradually fade although at times you may be troubled by memories that can be triggered by reminders of the traumatic event.

Recovery from trauma involves several things. Exercising thirty minutes daily can help your nervous system by releasing you from hyper-arousal. Connecting with others, especially those who can provide emotional support is helpful. Reengage with old friends or make new ones. Focus on your strengths. Calm yourself through breathing exercises, listening to music and doing other things that provide positive sensory input. Accept the feelings about the trauma but think realistically about them.

A healthy body increases your ability to cope with stress from a trauma. Be sure to get plenty of sleep. Lack of sleep can make symptoms worse. Eat a balanced diet. Use relaxation exercises to reduce stress.

Recovering from a traumatic event takes time. However, if months have passed and your symptoms aren't decreasing, you may need professional help from an expert in emotional or psychological trauma. Seek help for emotional or psychological trauma if you're having trouble functioning at home or work, suffering from severe fear, anxiety, or depression, unable to form close, satisfying relationships, having terrifying memories, nightmares, or flashback, feeling disconnected from others or using alcohol or drugs to feel better.

Post-Traumatic Stress Disorder (PTSD) is discussed here as it is related to trauma. It is an anxiety disorder that some people get after seeing or living through a dangerous event. It triggers many changes in the body to prepare to defend against the danger or to avoid it. This is called a "fight-or-flight" response. It is a healthy reaction meant to protect a person from harm. In PTSD, this reaction is changed or damaged. People who have PTSD may feel stressed or frightened even when they're no longer in danger.

Anyone can get PTSD at any age. This includes war veterans and survivors of physical and sexual assault, abuse, accidents, disasters and many other traumatic events. Not everyone with PTSD has been through a dangerous event. Some people get PTSD after a friend or family member experiences danger or harm. The sudden, unexpected death of a loved one can also cause PTSD.

The symptoms of PTSD can be generally grouped into three categories: re-experiencing symptoms such as flashbacks, nightmares or frightening thoughts; avoidance symptoms such as: avoiding those places, events or objects that are reminders of the experience with guilt, depression or worry and losing interest in activities or trouble remembering the event; and arousal symptoms such as startled reaction, feeling tense, difficulty sleeping, and/or angry outbursts.

Hyper-arousal symptoms occur when a person's body suddenly kicks into high alert as a result of thinking about their trauma and usually are constant rather than triggered by a reminder of the event. They can make the person feel continually stressed and angry, making it difficult to do daily tasks, such as sleeping, eating or concentrating.

Children and adolescents' reactions to trauma and its symptoms may not be the same as adults. In very young children, the symptoms can include: bedwetting, difficulty talking, acting out and clinging. Older children and adolescents usually show symptoms more like those of adults. They may develop non-normative behaviors or feel guilty. It is important to remember that not everyone who lives through a dangerous event gets PTSD. In fact, most will not get the disorder, but if they do professional help may be necessary.

There are both risk and resilience factors in trauma. Risk factors are: a history of mental illness, seeing people hurt or killed, feeling extreme fear, limited or no emotional support and added stress after the event. Resilience factors that may reduce the risk include: seeking emotional support from others, joining a support group, developing an effective coping strategy and an effective response regardless of a feeling of fear.

All of the following for at least one month are required for a PTSD diagnosis: one re-experiencing symptom, three avoidance symptoms and two hyper-arousal symptoms and symptoms that interfere with daily life, such as school or work, socializing with friends or completing important things.

Cognitive therapy, exposure therapy and eye movement desensitization and reprocessing are treatment methods. Anti-anxiety medications and antidepressants can also ease symptoms of PTSD. A professional psychotherapist should be consulted. A psychiatrist may be consulted regarding medication.

According to Dennis S. Charney, M.D., of the Icahn School of Medicine at Mount Sinai and Steven M. Southwick, M.D., of Yale School of Medicine characteristics of resilience to trauma are: maintaining an optimistic but realistic outlook, facing fear (ability to confront one's fears), relying upon one's own inner moral compass, turning to religious or spiritual practices, seeking and accepting social support, learning from and imitating a sturdy role model, staying physically fit, staying mentally sharp, having cognitive and emotional flexibility (finding a way to accept that which cannot be changed) and looking for meaning and opportunity in the midst of adversity.

Chapter 19
Supportive Environment and Social Role Valorization

A supportive environment is one that protects a person from threats to resilience and overall development. It validates and encourages involvement and participation in whatever a person is doing. The term can be applied to a number of situations. For example, a family has a general set of goals, whether written or not, and a process to achieve them. The contributions of each member toward the end are recognized. When family members are validated and recognized they are motivated to be involved in the family process by helping others in the family achieve goals. They may contribute to the family income, engage in solving interpersonal conflicts and suggest ideas that improve the family's overall welfare. They are likely to be directly helpful to another family member and engage in a myriad of other ways of involvement and participation.

Just as the family, a business has a set of goa ls. In the presence of a supportive environment, the individuals in the business are validated as meaningful contributors to the business. Being validated means feelings are recognized and accepted without judgment. Recall that feelings are never good or bad or right or wrong. Persons who are validated are involved in the business achieving its goals and participating in that process. Similarly, a mental health agency has a set of goals relating to restoring the mental health and social functioning of its clients. When the clients are validated, they will become more involved in their treatment process and likely experience positive outcomes. Other examples of goal-oriented entities include churches, social organizations, neighborhoods and cities. Nearly everything a person does is affected by feelings of validation although multiple situations do not offer a supportive environment.

Our culture promotes competition. Success is often measured by the amount of money and goods one has. Driving the best car, living in the nicest neighborhood and wearing the most fashionable clothes are just a few of these measurements. In today's culture, we tend to distance ourselves from each other. Often people don't know their neighbors. Families living together, or in close proximity, are unusual. The urban environment and crowded conditions in large cities tend to promote individual striving. These and other factors detract from a supportive environment and are omnipresent within the framework of a very competitive culture.

A supportive environment for children is primarily supplied by the family. The quality of the attachment between the child and the primary attachment figure is a major issue. Emotional or physical separation from her, especially if it occurs early in the child's life, may result in an insecure attachment style. An insecure attachment style does not fit with a supportive environment and may contribute to dysfunction in the family system.

Children also are challenged to find a supportive environment in school. Often classes are large and discipline is a serious problem that interferes with teaching and learning. Every school has a parent-teacher conference schedule that many parents don't attend but should. Many schools have a parent association that parents should join. Whatever is said about federal and state funding of education, the major support for local school districts is local tax. These are your tax dollars and you have an opportunity to influence how they are spent. Remember that school and district administrators are eager to hear from parents. Most teachers welcome contact with parents and are willing to inform them about a child's progress. They are interested in sharing with parents such items as whether attendance is regular, homework is submitted, behavior problems or if a child is being bullied. School is a place where children at a young age are often first introduced to substance abuse. A supportive environment in the school, to which every parent can make a contribution, has the potential of preventing substance abuse.

Work places for adults may be very non-supportive environments. Often, members of administration and supervision have outlasted everyone else to end up in charge whether they should be or not. This can make working under such supervision very frustrating and there may be little one can do to change such situations. The temptation to drink alcoholic beverages or smoke marijuana in an effort to console oneself may occur. Choosing alcohol or casual drugs may not an appropriate choice if for no other reason than many companies conduct random drug tests and termination of employment could result. In addition, drinking too many alcoholic beverages or use of casual drugs can affect work performance which can be observed and may lead to termination or other sanctions.

Therefore self-assessment becomes important in establishing a supportive environment. Negative feelings may run high so thinking, rather than feeling, becomes essential. Remember one cannot feel and think at the same time. It is important to read the employee manual or personnel policy document and a job description to know exactly what is expected of work performance.

A significant aid in managing a difficult work environment lies in the strength one gains through a supportive environment at home. If one feels good as the result of being cared for at home, one can withstand considerable frustration at work. A positive self-assessment can help an individual not to make poor responses to frustration at work by choosing to abuse alcohol or casual drugs which can lead to addiction.

Experiences create neural pathways in the brain which are stored in the amygdala, the emotional center of the brain. These feelings seek to be expressed and often an individual's reaction is to behave in response to them. Because this behavior is based on anxiousness the individual may become overly suspicious about the reactions of others. Anxiousness about the self can make an individual uncomfortable because they believe others are responding to their behaviors in a negative way. As a result, some may find relief through a variety of dysfunctional behaviors.

Treatment programs are available for addictions. Most are inpatient lasting for 28 days. However, the recidivism (return) rate suggests that something may be missing. Substance abuse or addiction is viewed as a disease so persons being treated are thought of as "sick." In this case the term "sick" has a non-normative context and is likely to produce behaviors that lead to an indifferent, neglectful and/or rejecting response by others. Hence, the person in treatment once discharged returns to the previous environment where nothing has changed and they end up back in the same situation as before treatment.

A supportive environment featuring a connection with others is something to consider seriously in the overall planning of a strategy to combat addictions as well as to resolve many emotional disorders.

There are many parts to this problem so a comprehensive plan will likely have many pieces. Suffice it to remember how important a supportive environment is in helping an addict stop or in helping people to change non-normative behaviors. Love and care for the person and let them know they are important. Build self-esteem through kindness and inclusion and encourage positive social contacts. Even when they slip, avoid criticism. The results will be positive.

Larger issues such as poverty and racism are significant and worthy of attention. They are beyond the scope of this book which is to encourage individuals to think about their problems rather than giving in to their feelings. The emphasis should be to consider how one can promote the development of supportive environments. Such environments could make a difference in the quality of life for many people.

A major objective in our culture should be to create supportive environments for all social positions. To accomplish this, efforts have to be made to assure that positive social positions are encouraged and enhanced.

Behavior is the focus in judging a supportive environment. The rules for behavior must be fully understood in addition to the consequences for not following the rules. The roots for establishing this structure lie in the family. Parents need to guide children by establishing a structure for appropriate behavior that is required for a supportive environment. When this is accomplished, children learn right from wrong and how to use this awareness in managing their behavior outside the family such as in their interactions with other children and adults at school, in the neighborhood or other social settings. Children become adults and with appropriate training in behavior, the culture can change. Ask yourself what you are doing that can contribute to this cultural change.

A companion idea to supportive environment is known as Social Role Valorization (SRV). This concerns how some groups and individuals are devalued because of their social position and social role behaviors. While SRV may be a new term for some, it is a concept that is important to consider as it is prevalent within the American culture. SRV replaced the principle of normalization which related to mentally retarded people who were perceived to be devalued and could not have access to the good things in life.

Today, we know the mentally retarded as being developmentally disabled or intellectually limited since these terms have less stigma attached to them.

Normalization is an idea developed in Scandinavia after World War II. The principle became law in Sweden so the good things in life that were available to persons in the mainstream would be equally available to all. Later this principle was introduced in the United States and applied to human services for all persons perceived to occupy devalued social positions. The goal was to establish cultural norms that would establish and maintain valued social positions and social role behaviors. SRV is a social science concept because it emphasizes what has to be done to improve the situation for persons in devalued social positions.

Several groups are perceived to occupy devalued social positions. Among these groups are criminals, the mentally ill, welfare recipients, the elderly, the intellectually limited and the homeless. Additionally, some people may be devalued because of their gender, sexual orientation or some other reason that causes them to be devalued by work or social groups.

Devaluation is society's view of those persons who have characteristics which place them in social positions that are regarded as having low value. Persons viewed as having low value often are treated the way they are perceived. They tend to live in lower quality housing, attend lower quality schools, have lower paying jobs and lower prestige jobs. Because of their status, they also tend to receive poor quality health care, receive assistance from established private and public systems that are perceived to be aiding persons of low value. The end result is that these individuals tend to perceive themselves as having low value. Negative self-perception may result in inadequate behavior in adaptation and social functioning. The observations of others then become critical in determining a person's value.

Judgment of the value of a person's social position using the perception of behavior as a criterion has ethical implications. The problem occurs when judging the value of a person's social position results in judging the person as either good or bad. The behavior of the person and not their social position is what can be judged. Unfortunately negative judgments often prevail.

When we see persons in so-called low value positions behaving in ways we don't accept, the feeling conveyed is negative and rejecting. These judgments are flawed. We need to think that every human has worth and work to help those in perceived low value positions be seen this as having value. View every social position on a horizontal plane rather than one that is vertical and it will become easier to detect differences in positions and role behaviors without judging their worth. Remember feelings are never good or bad or right or wrong. The same is true of social positions. This thinking can change the perception of the position. The response of persons in any position that is not judged negatively is to feel valued. This can contribute to a positive change in behavior.

Human service agencies are viewed as having the primary contact with low valued people. Using the concepts of social position and social role behavior, as described in Social Role Theory (SRT), to change perception might be helpful. For example, a community agency providing services to persons with serious and persistent mental illness used Social Role Theory as a basis for helping clients move from the devalued social position of mental patient to a valued social position in the family or the community. This was accomplished by continuously focusing on changing a client's mental patient social position and social role behaviors to normative behaviors that are acceptable to observers. In this agency emphasis was placed on helping clients locate volunteer or work and social positions where normative behavior was expected. This type of agency system supports SRV.

If SRV was similarly implemented in all human service systems, it could have an impact on consumers. Also, enhancing the image of these services would affect the perceived value of consumers. This can include the location of the service and such ambiance factors like the waiting room decor , how people are called for their appointment and the receptive non-judgmental attitude of providers. The primary effort of the provider should be to increase the appropriate use of the services by the consumer.

These ideas are presented with the knowledge that at least some readers are involved in human service systems such as mental health or financial assistance. It is important to remember that you are the consumer and you deserve good customer service. Don't be intimidated by any provider. If necessary ask to talk to a supervisor and remember to make sure you are given something in writing. A policy that affects you and that cannot be given to you in writing doesn't exist.

Feeling devalued can happen in other contexts. For instance, if you don't like your job, don't feel appreciated by friends and are living in a dysfunctional family setting, you may feel devalued. Similarly, if you have a history of struggling economically or have self-esteem issues because of inadequate attachment to a primary attachment figure you also may feel devalued.

At times, it's difficult to be objective or even simply realistic when your feelings are devalued. Every person has a need for personal relationships. Often these relationships can be disappointing if they are formed at work, especially when one has spent a significant amount of effort cultivating them. If relationship issues are a problem, perhaps you need to figure out what can be done to improve them through self-examination. This includes examining what feelings one is bringing to the job from other conflict arenas. Ask yourself what value you place on the job and how that is expressed in your attitude toward it and your fellow workers. Examine how you feel about your supervisor. Examine your feelings for the answers to these questions. It is easy to feel devalued in negative situations but making an objective evaluation may change your view. Think about the feelings and their source. What are the facts? Are the feelings accurate or are they distorted by a personal interpretation? It could be that you are creating your own negative sense of value.

Do you have confidence in how well you are doing the job? Do you feel competent to complete what you do? What is the content of your employment reviews? If you don't get a regular job performance review, ask for it so you can make adjustments if there are tasks for which improvement is needed. If you don't feel confident or competence in your work performance you may have a history of devaluing experiences. These may make you more vulnerable. It may be helpful to get professional assistance.

Living in a dysfunctional family setting may contribute to a likelihood that negative feelings can transfer from that setting to relationships outside the family. The source of negative feelings must be assessed as these can lead to feelings of being devalued. Examine the level of indifference, neglect and rejection between and among family members. It can take a lot of patience and acceptance of feelings to find the facts. However, when the feelings are uncovered thinking realistically about them can contribute to solving problems.

Social Role Theory (SRT) may be also helpful with problem solving. Ask what the role behaviors of the social position each family member holds. Are these behaviors in conflict? How do parents relate to each other? How do they relate to their children? Is there a sense of family unity? Is there an understood set of rules for behavior? Using Social Role Theory can make investigation clearer. Engaging in this process has the potential of increasing a sense of value among participants.

Thinking about feelings is the idea because thinking changes the whole perspective on relationships and in managing indifference, neglect and rejection. There may be times when professional help is required. The good news is that there are many sources for this assistance.

Many individuals face a difficult economic situation that may be serious and contribute to feeling devalued. Finding another job may be the answer but this change is demanding. Taking a second job sometimes works but there is a price to pay in longer hours and energy output. Some organizations offer internal training for those seeking advancement and some others pay for external training. Approaching the Human Resource Department may lead to such an opportunity. Whatever your situation, stay focused on thinking about positive actions. Giving in to devalued feelings does not help. Finding a support group of people with similar issues and concerns can be very helpful.

Remember, your own issues with self-esteem may be interfering with feeling valued. Examine your beliefs about yourself as these can affect the venues in your life. People develop a core belief about themselves mostly based on their experience with caretakers. If one feels accepted by primary caretakers and by one's family because messages of care and reassurance that are consistently received, these feelings can become a clear definition of positive worth. This process can form the foundation of a positive self.

When acceptance and care are not provided by attachment figures one may end up feeling that something is seriously flawed about self. This may lead to a negative self. This core negative self can generate negative feelings about self that can affect adaptation and social functioning. If you feel you are not worthwhile you also will feel that others perceive you as not being worthwhile and you will not be happy.

If one thinks about it and recognizes that what was learned can be unlearned and replaced with a positive self, life can be more settled. There are many family and social situations that contribute a negative self. Self-examination of your behavior that has contributed to the process

Chapter 20
Obtaining Professional Mental Health Assistance

This chapter discusses the mental health services that are available for those who may need them. It also presents information about when one should consider consulting a mental health provider and who might be an appropriate choice. Mental health services are becoming more widely available related to the federal government's concern and authorization of programs and funding for their operation. Most state and county government bodies share this concern. A network of services is available.

Federally Qualified Health Centers have been established in most areas in a state. These Health Centers care for you even if you do not have health insurance. Payment is based what you can afford. They provide checkups when you are well, treatment when you are ill, care when you are pregnant, and immunizations and checkups for children. Some also provide mental health, substance abuse, oral health, and/or vision services. The Health Resources and Services Administration (HRSA) is the agency of the U.S. Department of Health and Human Services that administers FQHCs. HRSA has a locator for these agencies on your personal computer.

State governments have health and mental health departments that create and manage local county programs for health and mental health services. Funding for these services is a combination of federal, state and county governments. Services are available at no charge for those who qualify. There is a range of private agencies that are funded by United Way or religious based institutions that may be consulted. For information about the location of any of these services there is a nationwide telephone connection by dialing 211. In an emergency or if you have no idea about where to start go to the emergency department of any general hospital where help will be available immediately.

Deciding when to seek mental health services is important. Those individuals who are troubled by mental or emotional problems may seek assistance on their own. However, there are many instances when another observer, generally a family member, will have to be involved because the distressed person is unaware of their symptoms and distressed behavior or because of denial of such a condition.

It takes courage to consult a mental health provider. Some are embarrassed over having an emotional problem believing it is a sign of weakness. Public stigma often affects people who experience these problems. Many times individuals blame themselves for having a mental illness which may cause them to not seek help. It is very important if you know a person who is having a mental upset to be supportive and non-judgmental. Encourage them and go with them if necessary to a mental health provider. It may be helpful to remind them that neuroscience- a study of the brain - has established the fact that neuropathways and neuronetworks in the brain that were created by negative or traumatic emotional experiences are the source of mental distress. This means an emotional disorder is really no different than a physical disorder except for the physical location of the malady in the brain that is an organ similar to other organs such as the heart and lungs. The major point to be made is to seek mental health assistance as soon as one recognizes an emotional upset. Similar to any physical illness early diagnosis and treatment makes a big difference in recovery.

It is generally believed that mental illnesses can be divided into three categories: *neurotic,* such as anxiety, depression, obsessive-compulsive disorder and phobias; *psychotic,* such as schizophrenia, bipolar disorder and major depression; and *organic illnesses* such as those associated with brain injury or disease or those produced by alcoholism or substance abuse. Anxiety is an emotional disorder that affects many people. There is generalized anxiety disorder, panic attack, obsessive compulsive disorder, phobias and post traumatic stress disorder (PTSD). Symptoms are numerous and vary depending on the type of anxiety. Some symptoms are mild and some more pronounced. Anxiety is not classified as a serious mental illness although it may be quite disabling. Almost everyone will experience anxiety of some type but if it does not interfere with social functioning there may not be a need to seek treatment. The multiple symptoms of anxiety are presented on your personal computer. Readers may be surprised to learn what some of them are because many are common and do not seriously effect functioning. However, they are an indication of underlying feelings that may at some point generate enough force to suggest consulting a mental health professional.

Depression is another quite common emotional disorder. Major depression interferes with a person's ability to work, sleep, eat, and enjoy pleasurable activities. Depression often follows a stressful event such as the death of a loved one. The cause of depression is not clear. Genetics and a stressful environment or life situation contribute to its cause or sudden onset. Some of the symptoms are unexplained crying spells, changes in appetite and sleep patterns, unusual sadness, irritability, anger and worry, agitation, pessimism, loss of energy, feelings of guilt or worthlessness, inability to concentrate, social withdrawal and recurring thoughts of death or suicide. There are different types of depression: major depression, persistent depressive disorder, bipolar disorder, seasonal affective disorder, psychotic depression, postpartum depression, dysphoria, situational depression and atypical depression. Children or teens may present with symptoms different from adults such as social withdrawal, unexplained aches or pain and irritability. A licensed, qualified mental health professional can make the diagnosis among the types.

The major point here is that all types of anxiety and depression are treatable. New medications are available and psychotherapy delivered by a qualified professional also may be very effective. Most private health insurance covers mental health issues. For those who do not have health insurance private and public mental health agencies exist in almost every geographical area. Your primary care physician may prescribe an appropriate medication for one of these neurotic illnesses. That may be a temporary answer. Sooner rather than later you will want to see a mental health professional. As suggested previously information about these agencies is available at telephone 211. It is important to note that talk treatment, either counseling or psychotherapy, provided by a licensed and qualified mental health professional, has the same effect on the chemistry of the brain as medication.

There is a group of serious and persistent mental illnesses (SPMI) including: schizophrenia, bipolar disorder and major depression. Schizophrenia is an illness that affects over two million or about one percent of American adults, the population age 18 and older.

Although often feared and misunderstood, it is a treatable condition. The major symptoms are problems with clear thinking, an inability to test reality, manage emotions, make decisions or have positive interpersonal relationships. There are three symptom categories: *positive*, such as delusions or unreal ideas about self or others and hallucinations (hearing or seeing things that are not there); *negative*, such as faulty speech, emotional flatness and lack of ability to experience pleasure; and *cognitive* such as disorganized thinking, memory problems and lack of insight.

Schizophrenia typically appears in the teenage years or early twenties, often later for females. Most people who have schizophrenia experience it chronically or episodically throughout their lives. They are often stigmatized by lack of public understanding. Schizophrenia also affects mood. Schizoaffective disorder may be diagnosed when the elements of schizophrenia and mood disorders occur together. The cause of schizophrenia is unknown. Research has shown that the actual brains of people with schizophrenia are different from those of people without the illness. Schizophrenia seems to be caused by a combination of problems including genetic vulnerability and environmental factors that occur during a person's developmental years.

There is no cure for schizophrenia but it is treatable and manageable. People sometimes stop treatment because of medication side effects, because they feel the medication is no longer working or because they feel better. This creates a risk of relapse into an acute psychotic episode. If you or someone you know is being treated for this illness continuing the medication is essential. Research shows that people with schizophrenia who participate in psychosocial rehabilitation programs and continue with their medical treatment manage their illness best.

Bipolar Disorder is a condition in which there are extremes in an individual's mood. It is characterized by the highs of mania to the extreme lows of depression. Another term for this condition is manic depression. The mood swings of bipolar disorder last for days, weeks or even several months. They are of high severity such that they impede routine functioning in varied ways. Despite this, it is difficult to diagnose bipolar disorder for its signs and symptoms may be rather subtle. But if diagnosed correctly, long-term treatment, which includes medication, external support and self-help, can allow a bipolar individual to live a normative life.

Here's a list of symptoms of bipolar disorder. *Manic Episode*: feelings of euphoria, abnormal excitement, or elevated mood; talking rapidly or excessively; needing less sleep than usual, yet having plenty of energy; agitated, irritable, hyper, or easily distracted feelings; risky behavior such as spending a lot of money, impulsive sexual contacts; poor business decisions.

Depressive Episode: loss of interest in previously enjoyable activities; loss of energy; sleeping too much or not at all; eating too much or not enough; *Major depression*, also labeled unipolar, or major depressive disorder, is characterized by a persistent feeling of sadness or a lack of interest in outside stimuli. Women are more affected than men by major depression.

Genetics is a prevailing cause of major depressive disorder. Co-occurring illness and medical conditions may be factors in a major depressive episode. Symptoms of the disorder itself can cause depression. Serious losses, such as loss of a job or death of a loved one also may be causes.

There are different types of *major depressive disorders*: seasonal affective disorder or SAD; psychotic depression; postpartum depression; melancholic depression; atypical depression and catatonic depression. Some symptoms are: negative thinking, agitation, inability to focus, lashing out, withdrawal, lethargy, suicidal thoughts and unusual loss or gain in weight.

Each of these illnesses is treatable. Recovery, defined as a state in which the illness no longer is a major factor in a person's life, is possible.

There are a number of classes of mental health providers. These include psychiatrists, psychologists, professional counselors, social workers, nurses and some family practice physicians who may write scripts for psychotropic medications and, if properly trained, may also provide counseling. Some ministers, priests and other religious professionals act as mental health providers. Only a few of them have the educational preparation similar to those trained to be practicing mental health professionals.

Psychiatrists are medical doctors who have education and training in psychiatry. Some are in private practice and some work in mental health clinics or mental hospitals. They are a primary resource for assessment and treatment of mental illness. They can prescribe appropriate medication and are a main pathway for hospital admission when it is necessary. Their involvement with a person who has a mental illness may be legally required in some instances. Other mental health professionals often seek consultation with a psychiatrist when they are providing psychotherapy.

Most health insurances have a behavioral health benefit. However, new laws and regulations in the health insurance industry have created co-pays and deductibles so you will want to check with your insurance provider or Human Resource administrator at your place of employment to learn what your employment benefit health insurance may cover. If there is a deductible that you have not met, you may have to pay out of pocket for services.

Psychologists are non-medical licensed mental health providers. They provide a variety of services such as psychometric and psychological testing and consultation, assessment and treatment of mental disorders. Psychometric testing mostly concerns a person's intelligence quotient (IQ). Psychological testing may reveal personality characteristics that are not apparent during an assessment interview. Knowing these characteristics may be very helpful in assessment and treatment of an emotional disorder. Some psychologists have a doctoral degree in psychology or education and some practice with a master's degree. Some have a private practice and some work in mental health clinics or public schools. Psychologists in private practice can be contacted directly for assessment or treatment. In some states psychologists can prescribe medication for mental disorders.

Social workers are licensed in most states to provide diagnosis and treatment of emotional disorders. In some states bachelor degreed social workers are licensed but their services do not include psychotherapy. Master degreed social workers provide most of the psychotherapy in the U.S. They work in a variety of public and private mental health agencies and hospitals. Some licensed master social workers have a private practice and are licensed to provide psychotherapy.

Some nurses have education and training in mental health practice. They may work in a hospital or mental health clinic or in private practice if they have an advanced degree. Some are licensed to prescribe medication along with psychotherapy.

You may want to inquire of your human resource department at work as to whether there is an Employee Assistance Benefit (EAP). Some companies contract with EAP health providers for mental health services. The number of sessions provided free is limited but often sufficient to solve a problem or get a referral for continued assistance that may be covered by health insurance.

Finally, it is important to have some idea about how well the mental health provider you've selected is doing to help you. Relationship is the key to success. If you feel comfortable with this person and believe she/he really cares about you then you probably have made a good choice. The next question is whether the provider has a knowledge base about the theory and practice of mental health assessment and treatment. You can tell this by whether you are learning about the reason for your emotional distress and whether you feel involved in the counseling or psychotherapy process. Is the provider asking the right questions to understand the problem? Do you understand the assessment the provider made about your condition? Have the two of you developed a treatment plan with objectives and goals? How will you know when treatment is complete? These are just some of the questions to ask. Counseling and psychotherapy consist of a meaningful conversation between two people with a focus on problem solving. It is important than the process feels good and that progress in resolving the problem is occurring.

Hopefully this chapter has provided some guidance about the mental health system. If you, or a family member, believe that an emotional problem exists don't hesitate to contact a mental health resource. Often your primary physician may be helpful with this decision.

Chapter 21
The Last Word

This chapter is a summary of the ideas and suggestions in this book that one may find helpful. The primary purpose of the book was to provide a way of resolving difficult emotional issues by *thinking* rationally and realistically about those events during a person's developmental years that generated assumptions and feelings about the self that were negative.

Chapter 1 offered a preview of the content of the book. In order to develop a base for how and what to *think* the contributions of some well known mental health experts were presented in Chapter 2. Further exploration of any one or all of these theories is encouraged. The knowledge one can acquire about the effect of developmental experience on the organization of personality enables *thinking* analytically about these experiences.

The application of theories was presented in Chapter 3 for the purpose of understanding how the thinking of experts in developmental psychology can be used by most people to find meaning in experience. This is especially relevant in the kind of *thinking* self-analysis that is recommended in this book. *Reflective thinking* can help a person uncover mistakes in assumptions and reactions to developmental events. The common theme of this explanatory approach was that childhood experiences are mostly responsible for how personality is formed.

Freud's psychodynamic theory, Erikson's psychosocial theory and Bowlby's attachment theory can be labeled as "explanatory theories" as each of them focuses on childhood developmental experiences as the foundation for the development of later emotional problems. Freud's theories were expanded in what is labeled "ego psychology" that resulted from Anna Freud's notion of the ego having its own energy. Melanie Klein, Heinz Hartmann and Margaret Mahler have significantly advanced this approach with object relations theory. In this approach the primary caretaker, usually the mother, also is the primary object meaning relationship figure.

A child's personality is shaped largely by the mother's nurturing care of the child. One of the main concepts in object relations theory is the ideas that the relationship between the primary object, usually the mother, is the basis for developing relationships with other objects (persons). The word object means the person toward whom positive associations or attachment feelings are directed. Father and siblings also play a role in a person's personality formation as secondary attachment figures.

Erikson's psychosocial developmental theory is similar except that its focus is on developmental milestones in the form of stage-related crises that must be resolved if the child is to develop a healthy personality. Bowlby's attachment theory is similar to object relations although he uses the term primary attachment figure rather than primary caretaker. He identifies the family members as secondary attachment figures and perceives the psychosocial environment as contributing significantly to personality development. Some people may think of his ideas as being similar to Erikson's approach. Bowlby borrowed ideas from object relations theory in forming attachment theory. Each of these theorists provides an explanatory way to think about how personality development can be flawed and lead to later problems with adaptation and social functioning.

These theories are useful in thinking about the negative emotional events of the developmental years because they help to explain feelings about these events and the assumptions about the self that were made as a result. It is negative assumptions that need to be reexamined as to their true meaning. Rethinking assumptions can result in seeing the circumstances of the events were responsible and not the self. That change in perspective will open a whole new and positive view and hay relieve guilt and self-blame.

Rogers and Maslow are included in the humanistic category of theorists that are focused more on the removal of roadblocks standing in the way of individuals achieving their desired goals. Unconditional regard for the individual is an essential ingredient. Glasser offers a similar perspective except that he proposes that the reality of a situation can control the outcome. In other words behavior has natural consequences that may lead to change.

Knowing something about Rogers' and Maslow's theories can be helpful in analyzing feelings associated with a sense of not having been viewed with positive regard. Knowing something about Glasser's theory may be helpful in reviewing the reality of developmental events.

Bandura and Skinner are from the behavioral theory tradition. They are concerned about behavior and its conditioning. These ideas are frequently used in institutional settings such as juvenile or adult corrections or mental health facilities. They are often successful in improving behavior although it is important that anyone receiving behavioral therapy services internalize the value of any change if it is to be long lasting. The benefit to knowing behavioral theory is gaining understanding of what feeling responses have been conditioned in life that are not helpful in positive adaptation and social functioning.

These comments briefly summarize the ideas of these theorists. More information about them and their ideas is available on the Internet and in the library. Hopefully readers of this book were helped to sense a direction about how to better manage emotional difficulties including the choice to seek professional assistance.

Spiritual power was the subject of Chapter 4. This was discussed for the purpose of acquainting readers with the power of the spirit and the strength that is available to *think* clearly about emotional problems. It was proposed that the soul, mind and heart are integral parts of the spirit of every human. This system has an eternal existence provided by God or a Supreme Power. This sharing of Divinity with humanity generates in humans a power of intellect and will that is available for solving emotional problems. This is an empowering concept.

Chapter 5 outlined a process for *thinking* consisting of *context, explanation and thinking* that one can use to rethink and relearn perceptions of emotional events. *Context* is the history of developmental experience including those of a crisis nature or trauma. *Explanation* is a phase during which learns reasons for emotional distress. *Thinking* is the rational application of what was learned in Explanation to rethink and relearn perceptions of distressing emotional experiences that can provide relief from distress.

Chapter 6 was about self-education and self-intervention. The purpose of this chapter was to further encourage self-education for self-intervention through the use of a process for thinking described in Chapter 5. The content is a social work theory based approach to Explanation and Thinking, the second and third phases of the process. Knowledge of theory is empowering. It encourages self-confidence in problem solving and provides a tool for thinking about emotions that is part of self-education.

A self-education process consisting of ideas from Attachment Theory, the subject of Chapter 8, and Cognitive Theory supplemented by constructivism and Vygotsky's Sociocultural Theory were described in sufficient detail for those readers seeking a self-help guide to mental health. Critical thinking about this combination of ideas organizes self- intervention. Ideas extracted from Cognitive Theory are methods leading to understanding the implications of Attachment Theory as applied to the self. Vygotsky's sociocultural theory and Constructivist Theory broadens this understanding.

Chapter 7 concerned critical *thinking* for self-awareness. Its purpose was to acquaint the reader with a method of *thinking* as a supplement to the information in Chapter 5. Critical *thinking* is based on a disposition to learn the truth about the effect of emotional experiences.

Chapter 8 was about attachment theory. This theory is one way to review how early child-parent and family relationships influence the development of feelings about the self and others. Attachment to a primary attachment figure is an inherent need in every child. Whatever characterizes this attachment will have a significant effect on personality development. Since memories of experience are stored in the brain there is a potential for a long term effect. These memories may be dormant until a similar event that may occur years later triggers recall and possible anxiety or depression.

Chapter 9 presented ideas about self-worth and the significance of this as a factor in achieving normative adaptation and social functioning. One needs only life to have worth. Worth may be determined by an accurate assessment of one's strengths and weaknesses. Realizing strengths and correcting weaknesses are important for mental health.

Chapter 10 focused on guilt and shame. These feelings were described and ways of managing them to bring relief from distress were suggested. Ideas were presented ideas about the concepts of guilt and shame as significant factors in emotional distress. Both were described along with suggestions about how to manage them.

Chapter 11 featured a discussion of anxiety, the mechanisms of defense and addictions. The word "anxiousness" was used in place of anxiety which is more of a diagnostic term while the term anxiousness better describes the state of mind for the anxious person. Addictions were included because so many people turn to social drugs such as marijuana, prescription drugs and alcohol as ways to "medicate" their anxiety.

Anxious feelings usually have a beginning early in a person's life. A child can internalize a negative sense of self if the child does not receive the level of care and nurturance required by its particular genetic system. This internal sense is expressed in anxiousness about the child's views of others' perceptions of her/him. If this is out of balance and the person is having more than average difficulty with adaptation and social functioning, the possibility of a more serious psychiatric illness should be considered.

Defense mechanisms contribute to maintaining the balance between the parts of the mind and reality. Their purpose is to control anxiety and the dysfunctional behavior that often accompanies it. Defenses are automatic and do not require thinking. However, defenses do not solve the problem that generated the anxiety in the first place but when they are successful, they may manage the anxiety well enough so the person can function reasonably. If the defenses are working then they are fulfilling their purpose and removing them suggests the underlying anxiety can emerge and emotional problems will reappear.

When the defenses are not working, consulting a mental health professional is advised. A professional has the knowledge and skill to assist in resolving the cause of the anxiety so the defenses are not necessary. Note that the effects of counseling or psychotherapy are typically not Instantaneous. It may take some time for treatment to be effective.

A common defense that people use to manage anxiety is to medicate with alcoholic beverages or illicit drugs. This almost always leads to worse problems especially since these substances may affect physical health and under some circumstances can cause death.

It is imperative to realize that when addiction becomes a problem it cannot be managed successfully without professional help.

Thinking works. Remember one cannot think and feel at the same time. For example, if one feels negative about self and has spontaneous negative thoughts, it is essential to *think* about whether these thoughts conform to reality or if they are "leftover" from child experiences from which erroneous assumptions were made about self-worth. Concentrate on a review of strengths including those many things that one does well and the many skills expressed in everyday living. If one focuses on the positive aspects of self anxiety can be reduced.

Chapter 12 described feeling and thinking and the distinctions between them. Often the behavior of people who have emotional problems is controlled by feelings. Thinking rationally about feelings can break the connection between feeling and behavior. One of the principal ideas of this book is that thinking about the accuracy of feelings is so important in constructing reality.

Chapter 13 was about mental functioning beginning with Freud's structure of the mind followed by Thomas Harris concept of child, parent and adult model. In this model, the parent is the rule setter and the reminder of what behavior is right or wrong. The child wants what it wants regardless of the rules. The adult is the mature and rational part that manages behavior largely as a mediator between the child and the parent. When the parent is rigid and unbending about judgments regarding behavior a child may become rigid regarding behavioral decisions and find it difficult to have a "good time." When the child is dominant, the individual is selfish and demanding and their behavior often is described as "childish." The adult is the mature thinking part of the mind. This theory is sometimes used by mental health professionals.

Included was a further discussion of neuroscience, a subject that has become more prominent because of the development of technology that has made understanding of the brain and its function much clearer. The subject of how the brain works in response to emotionally charged events and relationships can be explored by the average reader who will likely find the information very useful. The chapter concluded with some history of mental health service delivery and the contribution of the Chronic Care Model, another subject that many readers may find interesting and helpful.

Chapter 14 presented relationships that are an inherent need in all humans. Family, interpersonal, marriage and employment relationships were discussed. The capacity to form relationships is related to the nature of the relationship the individual had with the primary attachment object, usually the mother. The child gets a sense of a positive self from that relationship. The reasons why that sometimes doesn't happen are: the circumstances of the child's birth, the maturity of the mother, the quality of the mother's relationship with the father, separation from the mother for a period of time, the pressures on the mother for a variety of reasons such as several other children, mother's age and health, single parenthood or mother's employment and family economic circumstances. Factors that involve the child may also be significant such as premature birth, genetic deficit, attachment to the primary attachment figure, intellectual limitations and early abuse or neglect, especially sexual abuse. All these factors are important in an individual's developmental history as they affected the person's personality development and perspective on life.

The choice of relationships also is affected by the foregoing developmental issues. The saying "birds of a feather flock together" often applies to relationships. People who have an emotionally distressed developmental history tend to choose relationships with others who have had the same difficulties. Sometimes this happens because people who had negative developmental experiences believe they have an obligation to help others make a better adjustment. At other times a person's guilt over having internalized a negative self prompts them to soothe their guilt by depriving themselves for the good of others. This is a kind of self-punishment for a feeling of having been bad based on a false assumption.

The fact that the divorce rate is so high in this country suggests that many marriages were based on underlying neurotic needs that could not be satisfied through marriage. It is very easy to get married especially in this country. Some attempts at correcting this have been made, especially by churches, but nothing very effective has appeared to date.

Poor relationships can have a negative effect on health. Discouragement over an unhappy marriage, serious rejection from family members, loss through death and continuous frustration over a variety of issues may contribute to ill health. Depression often occurs for similar reasons and this can lead to unfortunate actions such as suicide.

Choose your friends carefully and your marital partners well. Guide your children regarding forming relationships. Keep the lines of communication open with them so they feel comfortable in talking with you about their friends and what is happening with them.

Chapter 15 presented person's stories about using the process for thinking described in Chapter 5. They were written in a way that readers may be able use the information to help themselves resolve many emotional problems without a counselor. Studying and applying this thinking process may clarify many of the mistaken assumptions made following difficult emotional events.

Chapter 16 is entitled "It's Not Your Fault." The main idea here is that the behaviors of primary and secondary attachment figures have a great impact on developing children. This same impact may occur from the behaviors of other children or adolescents. A problem arises when a child or adolescent blames themselves, feeling that there is a flaw in them that generated negative behavior in attachment figures. Such an assumption is erroneous and must be corrected. This assumption often is made because of fear that blaming a parent will make the situation worse. In almost every instance in which a parent is indifferent, neglectful or rejecting of a child there are reasons. These reasons may be traced to a parent's development history or other difficult psychosocial problems. In most cases it may be helpful in increasing parenting skills and positive family functioning if such a parent would seek mental health assistance.

The main point of this chapter is that others are responsible for indifferent, neglectful or rejecting behavior. Their behavior is not your fault. One of the major reasons for emotional distress is the erroneous assumption of self-blame, believing that a flaw in one's self is the reason for another's indifferent, neglectful or rejecting behavior. This is hardly ever the case.

Chapter 17 described how to get the most out of life and featured suggestions about ways to think and feel that may be helpful. It is important that a person develops a purpose in life and has objectives and goals one hopes to achieve. Several personality characteristics were identified as aids in achieving these objectives and goals and getting what one wants out of life.

Chapter 18 discussed crisis intervention and trauma. A crisis occurs when the ordinary problem solving ability of an individual doesn't work. Assistance from another person is required until the person in the crisis regains a balance and is able to manage the problem. Trauma usually is more difficult to manage. Suggestions about what to do were provided.

A supportive environment and Social Valorization were presented next in Chapter 19.

A positive social environment and a sense of acceptance or valorization are significant parts of achieving normative adaptation and social functioning. A comprehensive theme is how all of these factors affect the formation of feelings and the assumptions one might make about the self and others that contribute to emotional distress. Thinking rationally and realistically about both can generate change. Validation by your family of origin is very important in the development of self-esteem. Sustaining self-esteem for many people is made possible by a supportive environment. Whatever a reader can do to contribute to a supportive environment in the family, interpersonal relationships, and organizations such as churches, fraternal organizations, fellowship groups and businesses or any system where people congregate may be very helpful.

Chapter 19 is about resources that are available for persons who have a mental disorder. There are private and public agencies at which mental health providers are employed. The private agencies are sometimes sponsored by religious agencies. For example there are Catholic Charities that provide an array of services including mental health, marriage counseling and adoption and foster care. There also are many Christian Reformed, Lutheran and Jewish agencies that provide these services. There may be charge that behavioral health insurance would cover. Most of them have a flexible charge program. Services may be free for qualified persons.

Public agencies usually are administrated by counties in which they are located. There are federal and state funding programs managed by state health departments. Medicaid is the largest payer for services for those individuals who qualify. Currently there is a movement toward integrated care which means that both behavioral and physical health care is offered.

This final Chapter 20 summarizes the basic ideas of the book. Perhaps readers have learned about developmental history as affecting the course of one's life and a way that emotional problems may be resolved either by self or with the guidance of a professional. Thinking rationally about emotional problems may be very helpful. This book has provided the tools that most people can use to reexamine events in life that have generated anxiety or depression.

An important thing to remember is that children have sensitive reactions to the behavior of adults who are responsible for them. They learn very quickly from experience. When experience is indifferent, neglectful or rejecting the memories of them are stored in the brain. These memories may be easily triggered by events that occur later in life and interfere with normative adaptation and social functioning.

Attachment to a primary attachment figure is inherent in children. When attachment is flawed emotional problems may develop. Children who develop an insecure attachment style may find it difficult to relate to others. Their behavior may be noticeably dysfunctional. Withdrawal such as staying in one's room most of the time may occur. Communication with parents may be difficult. Sometimes acting out behavior such as temper tantrums or angry outbursts may be observed. Behaviors like these often will mean a child is emotionally distressed. These behaviors also may be observed in adolescents. In either case professional help should be sought. Pediatricians or primary physicians may be asked for help as they can refer parents to appropriate resources.

One last thought concerns the ability of counseling and psychotherapy to resolve the problems generated by the culture. Counseling and psychotherapy can help with responses to the challenges of life that often are due to issues beyond childhood, adolescent or adult interpersonal experiences. It is important to conclude a book on feeling and thinking with a reminder that all of us are related through being human and have a responsibility to each other in a global sense to make an effort to contribute to the resolution of major problems such as poverty, racism, inadequate educational programs, assisting the devalued to valued social positions, improving working conditions and opportunities and other similar concerns. These major social issues affect adaptation and social functioning but they are the subject matter of another book.

A Lagniappe

The term "mental illness "has been used because of the view that such illnesses occur in the brain however this does not recognize its physical properties

People who have a serious mental illness (SMI) also may experience self-stigma as well as public stigma. Often they are unable to find good jobs, appropriate health care and social acceptance. Self-stigma is different from public stigma. Self-stigma is an internalized sense of being bad or wrong. Public stigma is directed toward a particular group such as persons who have a mental illness. Both may decrease self-esteem.

Mental illness is perceived as such because people believe it occurs in the brain where the mind is thought to be by many people. However, the mind and the brain are not the same. The mind works through the brain but is separate from the brain. This does not negate the physical nature of the mind but rather suggests the mind needs a physical organ such as the brain to function.

The findings of neuroscience suggest that mental illness is physiological as neuropathways that are a physical record of negative emotional or traumatic experiences stored in the emotional center of the brain. The knowledge base of neuroscience is extensive and awareness of all its complexities is beyond the scope of this book. However, awareness of basic concepts can make a significant contribution to helping understand mental illness as a chronic health condition. Neuroscience produced evidence of neural plasticity that underlies the brain's ability to adapt and change in response to the environment This contributes to recovery from a mental illness, meaning that it is not a critical factor in a person's life.

The mind, which is the mechanism of expression of feeling, thinking and behavior that are characteristic of mental illness, is located in the brain. This is a central organ like the heart, lungs and the alimentary canal. It is the neural pathways in the brain that are the source of negative feelings that lead to disorganized thinking and behavior that form the symptoms that may be diagnosed as mental illness. What is really happening is that the anatomy of the brain has stored negative experience so the physiology or function of the brain affects behavior that is characteristic of mental illness. This process doesn't differ that much from the process of diagnosing a chronic physical illness. It is quite well established that a close connection exists between chronic behavioral and physical conditions so they should be categorized under a mutual heading such as chronic conditions.

The conceptualization of the term "mental illness" has to be changed in the public mind. Because of the custom of using the term mental illness, deleting it from everyday language may be a challenge. Various educational strategies may be effective in presenting facts about mental illness such as its physical properties.

Changing the terms physical and mental Illness and labeling them chronic conditions should be a goal.

There are several ways of thinking about reconceptualizing "mental" illness. Some mental health providers believe that attachment to a primary attachment figure is necessary to avoid later emotional distress. A way to reduce stigma is through generating public policy that assists all mothers in responding positively to children's need for attachment to them as primary attachment figures is possible. Achieving this would require assistance from a federal legislator. Attachment relationships that have failed such as with parents or a spouse may be refreshed or reconstructed with appropriate intervention.

A client's attachment to a mental health professional can change attachment style from insecure to secure. This is a significant concept for mental health providers to be aware. When persons with a mental illness have positive attachment relationships with others who do not respond negatively to the illness it is more likely that they will not self-stigmatize. Persons that have a mental illness should have regular interaction with others to show that mental illness is not as disabling as many people believe. Helping persons who self-stigmatize consist of initially making them aware that stigma is a public phenomena and is not a flaw in them. A group approach is proposed in which discussion occurs about how public attitudes are internalized by those who self-stigmatize.

Understanding this process enables these persons to understand how it develops and think differently about themselves as a result.

The Internet has other references for ideas about combating stigma that may be consulted by those interested in doing their part to decrease stigma. There are several other proposals about methods of combating stigma. The proposal, that merging the terms chronic physical illness and chronic mental illness into simply chronic condition, should be considered.

There are mental health service agencies available in almost every community in the country. However, few of them are engaged in educational programs for their clients or for the communities in which they are located. Such programs could be very helpful in combating stigma. Mental health agencies have a funding stream through a centralized system. For example, there is a Federally Qualified Health Agency in most areas in the United States. The central agency that funds the local agencies communicates with them regularly with policy statements, newsletters or other means. These methods should focus on presenting correct information about mental illness, especially that all such conditions are treatable and recovery, meaning the illness is not a major factor in a person's life, is available. New medications and advances in neuroscience about the physiological base of mental illness should be shared with the public. These systems could promote the language change in reference to chronic illness simply by using the term chronic condition repeatedly.

Every state has a health or mental health department, or a department that combines the two. There is a communication pathway between state and county offices where local programs are coordinated. It is proposed that the state departments could use this system to emphasize appropriate and helpful information about mental illness to all county agencies. For example, the state with which this author is familiar is divided into regions. Some highly populated counties stand alone while in several situations multiple counties are joined. Regions have central offices that provide services directly. There is at least one county that contracts with local agencies to provide specific services. There is an association of directors of public mental health agencies. This is a vehicle through which information about mental health could be passed.

Another community system that plans and funds social services that often include mental health care is United Way. This system is generally guided by influential members of the community who advise on policy and operations. The United Way planning group could appoint a task force to study the best way to establish a community system the main focus of which would be on educating the community about mental illness, especially its physical characteristics. This task force could study and make recommendations for employment of people who have a mental illness. Local agencies are where programming based on incoming information is coordinated. Here is where the action takes place, as clients are directly involved as recipients of services. It is proposed that these agencies develop psycho-education programs in which clients are given information about mental illness especially directed at combating self-stigmatization.

Similar psycho-education programs could be offered by these agencies at sites different from that where services are provided. Agencies and their personnel would be seen as involved as members of the larger community. These agencies also could organize a speakers' bureau to give talks at various clubs, organization, associations and business groups that are seeking speakers for their meetings. Local newspapers could be invited to have stories about these activities. Local radio and TV outlets might also be interested in broadcasting information about these events that would bring attention to the topic of mental illness that would encourage more general conversation among community members about the topic.

Leadership has to be provided by national membership organizations of professionals that regularly interact with persons who have a mental illness. The American Medical Association, the American Bar Association, the American Nurses Association and the Visiting Nurse Association could focus attention on education of their members about mental illness. This is especially recommended for non-psychiatric medical personnel who oppose the biological base of mental illness. It also is suggested that the curricula of Schools of Social Work include information about mental illness and the damaging effect of stigma on persons who have such an illness. Emphasis should be placed on recovery and strategies to achieve it.

These are some additional suggestions about what individuals can do to combat stigma. This is not an exhaustive list as many other ideas may occur to people as they think about this issue. The initial action is to learn as much as possible about what mental illness really is as an adjustment to very difficult circumstances that usually have involved rejection, indifference and neglect. These negative experiences form neural pathways that influence feeling, thinking and behavior. If you are a professional mental health worker equip yourself with correct information about mental illness so you can influence the system from the inside to develop programs that combat stigma. If you are a non-psychiatric physician or health services provider learn the anatomical and physiological aspects of mental illness as this will make a difference in how you relate to persons who have a mental illness. Learn about recovery from mental illness. It is not a permanent disability as with appropriate treatment recovery, meaning the illness ceases to be a major factor in a person's life is possible and even likely. As you learn more about mental illness you will become more empathy for persons who have it and will express this positive feeling in your contacts with them and others.

Don't differentiate chronic physical illness from chronic mental illness. Just refer to both as chronic conditions with no reference to type. Individuals could write their federal senator or representative and ask for sponsorship on legislation that would require dissemination of this information. Personal contact or telephone calls also are effective. Letters to state mental health boards also are helpful. Also contact county government individuals, especially those that serve on the board of the mental health agency, and request them to consider programs for clients and the community that combat stigma.

Mental health agencies often are seeking board members who are interested in policy formulation and implementation of service programs. You can find a way of becoming involved in the mental health system as a volunteer. Most United Way programs have a volunteer placement program. You can become a speaker advocate to combat stigma. Business associations always are seeking speakers at their meetings. Finally, we want to share information about the program we have chosen as one way to attack the stigma of mental health

Finally, I want to share information about an educational program that has a potential for expansion nation-wide. One organization, the

Mental Health Foundation of West Michigan, has spent over three decades focusing on building sustainable communities that support and understand mental illness. The MHF has created programs that equip individuals with the knowledge to recognize, understand, accept and take action when it comes to mental health. The organization's flagship program is called **be nice.**

be nice. is an upstream mental health and suicide prevention education

Program that has an action plan When the action plan is used effectively people have a

greater understanding of mental health, mental illness and suicide and are confident to start a conversation with persons perceived to have a problem.

Stigma is the number one reason someone struggling with mental illness or suicide doesn't speak up or reach out for help. **be nice.** is effective in increasing mental health awareness and a person's increased interest seeking help for a mental health concern. The program has an action plan for change at both micro and macro levels for any age.

At the micro level **be nice.** promotes recognizing depression and preventing suicide. At the macro level it promotes relationships that make it possible to talk about mental illness. Talking about the reality of the physical nature of this chronic illness will have the impact of increasing acceptance of the illness as most people do not stigmatize physical illness.

Reconceptualizing mental illness as a chronic physical illness was an objective of this chapter because the stimuli for emotional distress are neuropathways developed in the mind's emotional center by problematic emotional experiences that generally occur during developmental years. Viewing mental distress as arising from physical causes has the potential of considerably reducing stigma as physical illness and treatment are so much more acceptable to the average person.

Another objective was to establish the previously described **be nice.** educational program nationally. The long term plan is to contact all of the states' Department of Education about establishing **be nice.** in school districts in the state. If effective this could have an impact on perceptions of both mental health and stigma.

About the Author

Dr. Thomas J. Blakely was a clinical social worker and LMSW licensed by the state of Michigan. He is a Professor Emeritus of Social Work at Western Michigan University in Kalamazoo, MI.

After earning a Bachelor of Arts degree in Sociology from the University of Notre Dame in 1952 he began his career in the field of Social Work.

In addition to his Bachelor of Arts degree he earned three additional advanced degrees: In 1956 a Master of Social Work degree, in 1971 a Master of Arts in Education degree, and in 1975 a Doctor of Philosophy in Education degree. All were awarded from the University of Michigan.

Dr. Blakely has authored and published numerous articles on social work and mental health. After retiring from Western Michigan University in 1996 he continued a private practice in Clinical Social Work and Marriage and Family Counseling for which he was also licensed by the State of Michigan until his 91st birthday in 2022.

He currently resides in Belmont, MI with the love of his life for 70 years, Alice.

www.ingramcontent.com/pod-product-compliance
Lightning Source LLC
LaVergne TN
LVHW041710070526
838199LV00045B/1281